TORAH STUDIES

JEWISH LEARNING INSTITUTE

ב"ה

Season Four 5777

Student Manual

The ROHR JEWISH LEARNING INSTITUTE
gratefully acknowledges
the pioneering support of

George & Pamela
Rohr

Since its inception,
the JLI has been
a beneficiary of the vision,
generosity, care, and concern
of the Rohr family.

In the merit of
the tens of thousands of hours
of Torah study
by JLI students worldwide,
may they be blessed with health,
Yiddishe nachas from all their loved ones,
and extraordinary success
in all of their endeavors.

דוד שמואל בן זלמן גרשון ז״ל

David Shmuel ben Zalman Gershon ז״ל

*May the merit of the Torah studied in his memory
accompany his soul in the world of everlasting life,
and be a source of blessings for his family.*

Clive and Zoe Rock

*With deep appreciation for their leadership and partnership
with JLI in bringing Torah study to all corners of the world.*

*May they go from strength to strength and enjoy
good health, happiness, nachas from their loved
ones, and success in all their endeavors.*

Contents

1

MATOT-MASEI

No Wrong Turn

Each Person's Individual Mission

Dedicated in honor of our dear colleague and member JLI's Executive Board,
Rabbi Yosef Simcha Gansburg. *May he and his family merit to witness the fulfillment of continuous blessings for health, happiness, nachas and success in all their endeavors.*

PARASHAH OVERVIEW
Matot-Masei

Moses conveys the laws governing the annulment of vows to the heads of the tribes of Israel. War is waged against Midian for their role in plotting the moral destruction of Israel, and the Torah gives a detailed account of the war spoils and how they were allocated amongst the people, the warriors, the Levites and the high priest.

The tribes of Reuben and Gad (later joined by half of the tribe of Manasseh) ask for the lands east of the Jordan as their portion in the Promised Land, these being prime pastureland for their cattle. Moses is initially angered by the request, but subsequently agrees on the condition that they first join, and lead, in Israel's conquest of the lands west of the Jordan.

The forty-two journeys and encampments of Israel are listed, from the Exodus to their encampment on the plains of Moab across the river from the land of Canaan. The boundaries of the Promised Land are given, and cities of refuge are designated as havens and places of exile for inadvertent murderers. The daughters of Tzelafchad marry within their own tribe of Manasseh, so that the estate which they inherit from their father should not pass to the province of another tribe.

The Travels

TEXT 1

Bamidbar (Numbers) 33:1-33:6

אֵלֶּה מַסְעֵי בְנֵי יִשְׂרָאֵל אֲשֶׁר יָצְאוּ מֵאֶרֶץ מִצְרַיִם לְצִבְאֹתָם בְּיַד מֹשֶׁה
וְאַהֲרֹן:
וַיִּכְתֹּב מֹשֶׁה אֶת מוֹצָאֵיהֶם לְמַסְעֵיהֶם עַל פִּי ה' וְאֵלֶּה
מַסְעֵיהֶם לְמוֹצָאֵיהֶם:
וַיִּסְעוּ מֵרַעְמְסֵס בַּחֹדֶשׁ הָרִאשׁוֹן בַּחֲמִשָּׁה עָשָׂר יוֹם לַחֹדֶשׁ הָרִאשׁוֹן
מִמָּחֳרַת הַפֶּסַח יָצְאוּ בְנֵי יִשְׂרָאֵל בְּיָד רָמָה לְעֵינֵי כָּל מִצְרָיִם:

These are the journeys of the children of Israel who left the land of Egypt in their legions, under the charge of Moses and Aaron.

Moses recorded their starting points for their journeys according to the word of G-d, and these were their journeys with their starting points.

They journeyed from Ramses in the first month, on the fifteenth day of the first month; on the day following the Passover sacrifice, the children of Israel left triumphantly before the eyes of all the Egyptians.

Question—Why not "Encampments"?

TEXT 2

Rabbi Moshe Alshich, Bamidbar ad loc.

שמא תאמר, למה אמנה המסעות ולא החניות... ואם כן היה ראוי יאמר אלה חניות בני ישראל סוכות.

One can ask, why count the journeys and not the encampments... It would have made more sense to say "these are the encampments of Israel... Succoth, etc."

Nuance in Language

TEXT 3A

Shemot (Exodus) 40:38

כִּי עֲנַן ה' עַל הַמִּשְׁכָּן יוֹמָם וְאֵשׁ תִּהְיֶה לַיְלָה בּוֹ לְעֵינֵי כָל בֵּית יִשְׂרָאֵל בְּכָל מַסְעֵיהֶם:

For the cloud of G-d was upon the Mishkan by day, and there was fire within it at night, before the eyes of the entire house of Israel in all their journeys.

Rashi explains:

**Rabbi Shlomo Yitzchaki
(Rashi)**
1040–1105
Most noted biblical and
Talmudic commentator.
Born in Troyes, France,
Rashi studied in the famed
yeshivot of Mainz and
Worms. His commentaries
on the Pentateuch and
the Talmud, which focus
on the straightforward
meaning of the text, appear
in virtually every edition
of the Talmud and Bible.

TEXT 3B

Rashi, ad loc.

"לעיני כל בית ישראל בכל מסעיהם"... מקום חנייתן אף הוא קרוי
מסע, וכן "וילך למסעיו", וכן "אלה מסעי" לפי שממקום החנייה
חזרו ונסעו, לכך נקראו כולן מסעות.

"*Before the eyes of the entire house of Israel in all
their journeys.*"... The place of their encampment is
also called a journey. Likewise, "And he went to his
stations" [i.e., to the stops along his journey], and
likewise, "These are the journeys." Inasmuch that they
resumed their journeys from the place of their encampment, they are all called "journeys."

Question—Journeys, Plural?

TEXT 4

Rabbi Shneur Zalman of Liadi, Likutei Torah Bamidbar 88c

להבין לשון "אלה מסעי" שהוא לשון רבים וכתיב "אשר יצאו
מארץ מצרים". והרי מארץ מצרים הוא רק יציאה ונסיעה ראשונה
שנסעו מרעמסס לסוכות?

The wording of the verse "these are the journeys" is puzzling. It is worded in the plural tense, yet it continues "that they left Egypt." Now, leaving Egypt was accomplished with the first travel, when they left Ramses for Succoth!

Rabbi Shneur Zalman of Liadi
(Alter Rebbe)
1745–1812
Chasidic rebbe, halachic authority, and founder of the Chabad movement. The Alter Rebbe was born in Liozna, Belarus, and was among the principal students of the Magid of Mezeritch. His numerous works include the *Tanya*, an early classic containing the fundamentals of Chabad Chasidism, and *Shulchan Aruch HaRav*, an expanded and reworked code of Jewish law.

Life as We Know It

The Journey of Life

TEXT 5

Ibid. 89b

והנה עיקר ותכלית נסיעתן היה לצאת מבחינת מצרים בחינת מיצר
וגבול... ולכן כל המ"ב מסעות נקרא הכל אשר יצאו מארץ מצרים
והיינו עד חנייתם בירדן יריחו.

Now, the overarching thrust of their travels was to leave behind that which Egypt represents, namely the aspect of constraint and limitation... Therefore, all of the forty-two travels are summarily termed "that they left from Egypt," up until their arrival at the Jordan River.

TEXT 6A

Moshe Chaim Efraim of Sudilkov,
Degel Machaneh Efraim, Bamidbar ad loc.

Rabbi Moshe Chaim
Efraim of Sudilkov
1748–1800

ששמעתי בשם אא״ז זללה״ה כי כל המסעות היו מ״ב והם אצל כל
אדם מיום הולדו עד שובו אל עולמו.

Chasidic teacher and author.
Rabbi Moshe Chaim Efraim
was a grandson of the
Baal Shem Tov, who took
a personal interest in his
education. After the Baal
Shem Tov's passing, he
studied under the Magid of
Mezeritch and Rabbi Ya'akov
Yosef of Polnoye. He later
settled in Sudilkov, where he
served as rabbi. His Chasidic
work, *Degel Machaneh
Efraim*, is a commentary on
the weekly Torah portions;
it was printed posthumously
by his grandson Rabbi
Ya'akov Yechiel of Kuritz.

I heard in the name of my holy grandfather, the Baal
Shem Tov, that a person experiences these 42 journeys
in their personal life—from the day he is born until the
day he dies.

TEXT 6B

Rabbi Menachem Mendel Schneersohn of Lubavitch,
The Tzemach Tzedek, Ohr Hatorah Masei p. 1352

Rabbi Menachem
Mendel Schneersohn
of Lubavitch
(*Tzemach Tzedek*)
1789–1866

הנה מארץ מצרים עד בואם אל ארץ ישראל ארץ טובה ורחבה הלכו
מ״ב מסעות. ואמרו רז״ל מזכירין יציאת מצרים בכל יום בקריאת
שמע שחרית וערבית, ובכל דור חייב אדם לראות את עצמו כאלו
יצא ממצרים, לכן יש בחינת מ״ב מסעות גם כן בכל יום.

Chasidic rebbe and noted
author. The *Tzemach Tzedek*
was the third leader of the
Chabad Chasidic movement
and a noted authority on
Jewish law. His numerous
works include halachic
responsa, Chasidic discourses,
and Kabbalistic writings.
Active in the plight of
Russian Jewry, he worked
to alleviate the plight of the
Cantonists, Jewish children
kidnapped to serve in the
Czar's army. He passed away
in Lubavitch, leaving seven
sons and two daughters.

The Jews underwent 42 journeys on their travels from
Egypt to the Promised Land. Our Sages state that it is
a mitzvah to remember the Exodus every day when
reciting Shema in the morning and evening, and he is
obligated to see himself as if he personally went out of
Egypt. Thus, there are 42 journeys every day.

Stopping Along the Way

TEXT 7

The Lubavitcher Rebbe, Likutei Sichot vol. 23 pp. 225-226

Rabbi Menachem Mendel Schneerson
1902–1994
The towering Jewish leader of the 20th century, known as "the Lubavitcher Rebbe," or simply as "the Rebbe." Born in southern Ukraine, the Rebbe escaped Nazi-occupied Europe, arriving in the U.S. in June 1941. The Rebbe inspired and guided the revival of traditional Judaism after the European devastation, impacting virtually every Jewish community the world over. The Rebbe often emphasized that the performance of just one additional good deed could usher in the era of Mashiach. The Rebbe's scholarly talks and writings have been printed in more than 200 volumes.

דער סדר הרצוי פון חיי האדם איז, אז ביי אים זאל שטענדיק זיין—
"מסע", ער זאל זיין א מהלך. ווי חסידות איז מבאר דעם חילוק
צווישן "עמידה" און "'הילוך" אין עבודת השם:

"עמידה" מיינט אז מען שטייט אויפן זעלבן ארט, אפילו ווען מ'איז
עולה צו א העכערער מדריגה, איז דאס נאר אן עליה בערך—די
העכערע מדריגה האט אן ערך צו (וממילא א שייכות ובמילא א
מעין פון) דער פריערדיקער מדריגה, ובמילא איז ער ניט "אוועק"
(לאמיתתו) פון זיין פריערדיקער מדריגה.

"הילוך" (לאמיתתו) מיינט: א הילוך ועליה שלא בערך אז מען
גייט אינגאנצן אוועק פון דער נידעריקער מדריגה, די העכערע
מדריגה איז א באין ערוך העכער פון דער מדריגה אין וועלכער ער
איז פריער געשטאנען...

און דערפאר זאגט דער פסוק "אלה מסעי", צו מרמז ומדגיש זיין,
אז א איד זאל זיך ניט אפשטעלן און בלייבן (חניה) ביים זעלבן
סוג עליה מדרגא לדרגא, נאר זיינע עליות דארפן זיין באופן אז די
צווייטע עליה ("מסע") איז אפגעטיילט, באין ערוך העכער פון דער
ערשטער, א הליכה מחיל אל חיל.

The ideal mode in which a person ought to operate is one of constant "travel." He or she ought to be constantly "moving," a reference to how the terms "stagnant" and "mobile" are explaind in Chassidic works in the context of Divine service:

"Stagnant" means that the individual is stuck in one place. Even when such a person does indeed graduate to a loftier state, it is still a measured graduation, inasmuch that the new state of being is closely related to the previous one. Accordingly, the person never really "breaks free" from his or her original status.

True "motion" means to graduate exponentially *from the previous state to a place that is entirely unrelated and removed from where the individual previously stood...*

For this reason, the verse states, "These are the journeys..."—to underscore the idea that a Jew ought not to grow in a measured "encampment" sort of way, rather his or her growth ought to look like this: The second journey *is entirely removed*, exponentially greater *than the previous* journey, *a true growth from* "strength to strength."

Guiding the Footsteps of Man

How Did I Get Here?

TEXT 8

Tehillim (Psalms) 37:23

מֵה' מִצְעֲדֵי גֶבֶר כּוֹנָנוּ וְדַרְכּוֹ יֶחְפָּץ:

From G-d man's steps are established, for He delights in his way.

G-dly Sparks

TEXT 9

Rabbi Chaim Vital, Eitz Chaim 26:1

Rabbi Chaim Vital
ca. 1542–1620

Lurianic Kabbalist. Rabbi Vital was born in Israel, lived in Safed and Jerusalem, and later in Damascus. He was authorized by his teacher, Rabbi Yitzchak Luria, the Arizal, to record his teachings. Acting on this mandate, Vital began arranging his master's teachings in written form, and his many works constitute the foundation of the Lurianic school of Jewish mysticism. His most famous work is *Ets Chaim*.

ואמנם ידעת גם כן כי כל המצות אינם אלא לצרף ולברר הצלם
והחומר אך הצורה אין צריך תיקון כלל ולא הוצרכה להתלבש
בצלם וחומר רק להמשיך בהם אור לתקנם והבן זה מאד. כי זה
טעם ירידת הנשמה בעולם הזה לתקן ולברר דוגמת גלות השכינה
לברר ניצוצין שנפלו כנודע.

It is known that the purpose of the mitzvot is to refine and sublimate the form and the material. The spirit itself does not need refinement; the only reason the spirit was compelled to integrate within a form and matter was to draw down a light that would rectify that matter. This is the reason the soul descended upon this world—to rectify and to sublimate it, similar to the exile of the Shechinah, which is to sublimate the G-dly sparks that have fallen.

The Secret of Eating

TEXT 10

Rabbi Yisrael Baal Shem Tov, Keter Shem Tov §194

Rabbi Yisrael Baal Shem Tov (Besht)
1698–1760
Founder of the Chasidic movement. Born in Slutsk, Belarus, the Baal Shem Tov was orphaned as a child. He served as a teacher's assistant and clay digger before founding the Chasidic movement and revolutionizing the Jewish world with his emphasis on prayer, joy, and love for every Jew, regardless of his or her level of Torah knowledge.

והמשל למלך שנאבדה לו אבן טוב מתוך טבעתו, והנה עמדו לפני המלך בעת ההיא הרבה מעבדיו ושריו הפרתמים והפחות והסגנים מאנשי מלחמתו עד אין מספר, עם כל זה לא רצה המלך לצוות להם שיחפשו אחר האבן טוב, רק צוה לבנו יחידו וחביבו שיחפש וימצא האבידה ויחזירנה לאביו המלך, הגם שהיה המלך בטוח מכל אחד משריו ועבדיו שכאשר ימצאנו יחזירנו בשלימות, אף על פי כן לא היה ברצונו שהם יחפשו כי רצה לזכות את בנו חביבו וכדי שיקרא המציאה על שמו.

ולא עוד, אלא גם רמז לבנו חביבו בכמה רמזים מקום מציאותו, כי מתחלה היתה האבידה מדעת המלך את מקומה ועשה הכל רק למען לזכות את בנו חביבו, וכדי שיגיע גם להמלך מזה גודל שעשוע והתפארות מבנו לאמר לאמר ראו כי שום בן אדם בעולם לא היה יכול לחפוש ולמצוא זולת בנו חביבו.

והנמשל מובן, שתחילת בריאת העולמות היה כדי לברר הניצוצין קדישין על ידי אומה ישראלית, כמו שנאמר "בשביל ישראל שנקרא ראשית", שעל ידם יבררו ממאכלים מותרים וכשרים.

וזהו שאמר ר' ישראל בעל שם על פסוק "רעבים גם צמאים נפשם בהם תתעטף", פירוש בכאן סוד גדול [ונורא], והוא למה ברא הקדוש ברוך הוא דברי מאכל ומשקה שאדם תאב להם [לאכול ולשתות]? והטעם שהם [ממש ניצוצות אדם הראשון שהם] מתלבשים בדומם צומח חי מדבר ויש להם חשק להדבק בקדושה, והם מעוררים מיין נוקבין בסוד אין טפה יורדה מלמעלה שאין טפיים עולים כנגדה, וכל אכילה [ושתיה] שאדם אוכל ושותה היא ממש חלק ניצוצות שלו שהוא צריך לתקן. וזהו שכתוב "רעבים גם צמאים", כשאדם רעב וצמא להם, למה זה, [וזהו שכתוב] "נפשם בהם תתעטף", בסוד גלות [בלבושי זרים] ויחשבה לזונה כי כסתה פניה, וכל הדברים שהם משמשין לאדם הם ממש בסוד הבניה שלו שהלבישו, והבן.

והשם יתברך רמז להם לישראל בכמה רמזים שימצאו האבידה ויחזרו לבעליהם, לאביהם שבשמים, ולא צוה כן למלאכים ושרפים ואופנים, והאבידה ההוא מדעת היתה כמאמר רז"ל שהיה בונה עולמות ומחריבן.

An analogy:

A king once lost a precious stone. All the important ministers, aides, officers, and military leaders were present, yet the king did not instruct them to find his precious stone; rather, he directed his instruction to his beloved only son. Though the king had complete confidence that his ministers and servants could surely find the stone and faithfully return it, he wished to bestow his beloved son with the great honor of being the one who successfully found the lost item.

What's more, the truth is that the king really knew where the stone was hidden. He engineered the whole ploy just to give his beloved son more opportunity, and to enjoy the immense pleasure of seeing his own son be the only one to find the stone. So, he even hinted to his son where the stone may be found.

The analogue is obvious: The entire purpose of why G-d created this world was so that the Jews could redeem the G-dly sparks, for the Jew can sublimate kosher and permissible food items.

The Baal Shem Tov revealed a fascinating secret hidden in the words of the verse "Hungry as well as thirsty, their soul enwraps itself in them." These words come to answer the question "Why did G-d create food items that man craves and needs to survive?"

The reason is that the Divine sparks of G-d are trapped in the various creations on earth. These sparks wish to cleave to holiness, so they call out and stir a response. Every time a person eats or drinks, he is sublimating these sparks that have called out and need refinement.

This, then, is the meaning of the verse, "Hungry as well as thirsty, their soul enwraps itself in them,"—Why is a person hungry or thirsty for food and drink? "Because of the soul that is trapped within them."

G-d hints to the Jew in various ways to find the lost object and return it to its rightful owner—their Father in Heaven. [As in the analogy,] G-d did not instruct the angels, and the loss was intentional.

Your Possessions

TEXT 11

Rabbi Dovber of Mezritch, Ohr Torah, Agaddot Chazal §413

Rabbi Dovber "the Magid" of Mezeritch
d. 1772
Was the primary disciple and eventual successor of the Baal Shem Tov. Amongst his disciples were the founders of various Chasidic dynasties, including Rabbi Nachum of Chernobyl, Rabbi Levi Yitzchak of Berditchev, and Rabbi Shneur Zalman of Liadi. His teachings, recorded by his students, appear in various volumes including the *Magid Devarav Leya'akov.*

התורה חסה על ממונם של ישראל. ולמה כך?

כי זה כלל גדול שכל דבר שאדם לובש או אוכל או משתמש בכלי, הוא נהנה מהחיות שיש באותו דבר. כי לולי אותו הרוחניות לא היה שום קיום לאותו דבר, ויש שם ניצוצות קדושות השייכים לשורש נשמתו.

(ושמעתי כי זהו הטעם שיש אדם שאוהב דבר זה, ויש אדם ששונא דבר זה ואוהב דבר אחר.)

וכשהוא משתמש באותו הכלי, או אוכל מאכל אפילו לצורך גופו, הוא מתקן הניצוצין. כי אחר כך עובד בכח הזה שבא לגופו מאותו מלבוש או מאכל או שאר דברים, ובזה הכח עובד להשם יתברך, נמצאו מתוקנים.

ולכך פעמים שיאבד הדבר ההוא ממנו. שכבר כלה לתקן כל
הניצוצין שהיו באותו הדבר השייכין לשורש נשמתו, אז לוקח ממנו
השם יתברך אותו הכלי ונותן לאחר ששייכין הניצוצות שיש באותו
הכלי לשורש [של] אחר [שהוא משורש נשמתו]...
לכך צריך אדם לחוס על כליו ועל כל דבר שיש לו, דהיינו מצד
הניצוצין שיש שם, בכדי לחוס על הניצוצין הקדושות.

[It is a halachic *principle that] "The Torah is compassionate with the monies of Israel." Why is this so?*

Know this broad rule: A person derives benefit from the energy contained within every item he eats, wears, or otherwise uses. Were it not for that spiritual energy, it would not exist.

Now, there are holy sparks in that item that relate exclusively with the soul of its owner, and when he or she uses or eats that item—even if only for bodily purposes—they redeem those sparks. For afterward, he or she serves G-d with those garments or with the energy from that food, thus sublimating the sparks trapped inside of them.

[I have heard that this is the reason why some people like certain items and despise others, while other people like those same items and despise different ones.]

For this reason, people will lose their money or personal articles. The owner has finished redeeming the sparks in that item that relate exclusively to his soul, so G-d takes it away and gives it to another person whose soul does relate to the remaining sparks in that item…

One must therefore be careful with his personal articles and possessions, that is, he should be mindful of the Divine sparks hidden inside them.

Your Place

TEXT 12

The Lubavitcher Rebbe, Hayom Yom, Entry for 10 Tamuz

רבינו הזקן בתחילת נשיאותו אמר תורה: מה' מצעדי גבר כוננו, אז א איד קומט אין א ארט, איז עס צוליב א כוונה טאן א מצוה, הן א מצוה שבין אדם למקום והן א מצוה שבין אדם לחבירו. א איד איז א שליח של מעלה, א שליח וואו ער איז, איז ער דער כח המשלח, דער יתרון המעלה אין נשמות לגבי מלאכים - וואס בא נשמות איז דאס על פי התורה.

In the early period of his leadership, the Alter Rebbe taught: "The footsteps of man are directed by G-d."

When a Jew comes to a particular place it is for an (inner Divine) intent and purpose—to perform a mitzvah, whether a mitzvah between a person and G-d or a mitzvah between a person and his or her fellow. A Jew is G-d's messenger. Wherever a messenger may be, he represents the power of the one who sent him.

The superior quality that souls possess, higher than the angels (who are also "messengers"), is that souls are messengers by virtue of Torah.

TEXT 13

Ibid., Entry for 3 Elul

המאמין בהשגחה פרטית יודע כי מה׳ מצעדי גבר כוננו, אשר נשמה זו צריכה לברר ולתקן איזה בירור ותיקון במקום פלוני. ומאות בשנים או גם משעת בריאת העולם הנה הדבר שצריך להתברר או להתתקן מחכה לאותה הנשמה שתבוא לברר ולתקנו וגם נשמה הלזו הנה מאז נאצלה ונבראה היא מחכה לזמן ירידתה לברר ולתקן את אשר הוטל עליה.

Whoever has faith in individual Divine Providence knows that "man's steps are established by G-d," that this particular soul must purify and improve something specific in a particular place. For centuries, or even since the world's creation, that which needs purification or improvement waits for this soul to come and purify or improve it. The soul, too, has been waiting—ever since it came into being—for its time to descend, so that it can discharge the tasks of purification and improvement assigned to it.

TEXT 14

Ibid., Entry for 5 Adar I

בלי שום צל ספק וספק ספיקא, בכל מקום מדרך כף רגלינו, הכל
הוא לזכות ולטהר את הארץ באותיות התורה והתפלה, ואנחנו כל
ישראל שלוחי דרחמנא אנו, איש איש כאשר גזרה עליו השגחה
העליונה, אין חפשי מעבודת הקדש, אשר הועמסה על שכמנו.

*There is not the vaguest shadow of doubt that wher-
ever our feet tread, it is all in order to cleanse and
purify the world with words of Torah and prayer. We,
all of Israel, are emissaries of G-d, each of us as Divine
Providence has decreed for us. None of us is free from
this sacred task placed on our shoulders.*

TEXT 15

Rabbi Yosef Yitzchak of Lubavitch, Igrot Kodesh vol. 3 p. 561

Rabbi Yosef Yitzchak Schneersohn
(Rayatz, Frierdiker Rebbe, Previous Rebbe)
1880–1950

Chasidic rebbe, prolific writer, and Jewish activist. Rabbi Yosef Yitzchak, the 6th leader of the Chabad movement, actively promoted Jewish religious practice in Soviet Russia and was arrested for these activities. After his release from prison and exile, he settled in Warsaw, Poland, from where he fled Nazi occupation, and arrived in New York in 1940. Settling in Brooklyn, Rabbi Schneersohn worked to revitalize American Jewish life. His son-in law, Rabbi Menachem Mendel Schneerson, succeeded him as the leader of the Chabad movement.

הנה כתיב מה' מצעדי גבר כוננו ודרכו יחפץ. כל אחד ואחד מישראל יש לו תעודה בחיים חיותו בעלמא דין בשביל להשלים הכוונה העליונה יתברך ויתעלה אשר איוה להיות לו יתברך דירה בעולם הזה הגשמי דוקא, ודירה זו עושים רק על ידי קיום המצות מעשיות לימוד התורה ועבודת התפלה, אשר זה הוא התעסקותם של כל ישראל לבנות הדירה, זה בכה וזה בכה, כל אחד ואחד כפי חלקו בעבודה זו על פי ההשגחה העליונה.

והנה מי אשר כלי פרנסתו הוא באופן כזה שצריך לעשות נסיעות. הנה עליו לדעת כי ענין חלקו בבנין הדירה לפני מלך מלכי המלכים הקדוש ברוך הוא הוא אשר בכל מקום היותו עליו לפעול איזה ענין בהרבצת תורה בחיזוק היהדות בשמירת שבת בקביעות עתים לשיעורי לימודים הן באמירת תהלים, והן באיזה לימוד בהלכה או אגדה בכל מקום ומקום לפי תנאי יושבי המקום ההוא...

וזהו מה' מצעדי גבר כוננו, לכל אחד ואחד מישראל יש תעודה רוחנית בחיים, והוא להתעסק בעבודת הבנין לעשות דירה לו יתברך, וכל אחד באשר הוא ובכל מקום שהוא צריך להתעניין בכל מאמצי כוחו לחפש בחפש מחופש למצוא איזה פרנסה רוחנית באחד העניינים בחיזוק היהדות בהרבצת התורה ובהתעוררות במדות טובות, כמו שהוא מחפש אחר פרנסה גשמית.

The verse states, "From G-d are man's steps established." Every Jew has a spiritual mission in life to fulfill the Divine desire to have a dwelling place in this material world. This home can only be constructed through studying Torah and fulfilling practical mitzvot. This, then, is the job of every Jew—each one building G-d's home in the particular corner of the world where Divine Providence has led them.

Now, if a person's business concerns compel him to frequently travel, he must know that his part in building G-d's home is to spread Jewish awareness and religious observance wherever his travels take him. He should encourage regular Torah study, reciting Tehillim, studying different areas of Torah—each place according to its individual style and needs…

"From G-d are man's steps established." Every one of Israel has a spiritual mission in life—which is to occupy himself with the work of construction, to make a "dwelling-place" for G-d. Everyone, regardless of his or her station or location, must, through an exhaustive search, seek out a spiritual livelihood with all the intensity of his strength, just as he or she seeks a material livelihood.

DEVARIM

Reparative Wreckage

Each Person's Individual Mission

Dedicated in honor of our dear colleague and member of the Torah Studies editorial board,
Rabbi Ari Sollish. *May he and his family merit to witness the fulfillment of continuous blessings for health, happiness, nachas and success in all their endeavors.*

PARASHAH OVERVIEW
Devarim

On the first of Shevat (thirty-seven days before his passing), Moses begins his repetition of the Torah to the assembled children of Israel, reviewing the events that occurred and the laws that were given in the course of their forty-year journey from Egypt to Sinai to the Promised Land, rebuking the people for their failings and iniquities, and enjoining them to keep the Torah and observe its commandments in the land that G-d is giving them as an eternal heritage, into which they shall cross after his death.

Moses recalls his appointment of judges and magistrates to ease his burden of meting out justice to the people and teaching them the word of G-d; the journey from Sinai through the great and fearsome desert; the sending of the spies and the people's subsequent spurning of the Promised Land, so that G-d decreed that the entire generation of the Exodus would die out in the desert. "Also against me," says Moses, "was G-d angry for your sake, saying: You, too, shall not go in there."

Moses also recounts some more recent events: the refusal of the nations of Moab *and* Ammon *to allow the Israelites to pass through their countries; the* wars *against the Emorite kings Sichon and Og, and the settlement of their lands by the tribes of Reuben and Gad and part of the tribe of Manasseh; and Moses' message to his successor,* Joshua, *who will take the people into the Land and lead them in the battles for its conquest:* "Fear them not, *for the L-rd your G-d, He shall fight for you."*

A Temple for One

Introduction

Rabbi Yehoshua Falk Hakohen Katz
1555–1614

Polish rabbi, Talmudist, and authority on Jewish law. Rabbi Falk is best known for his *Perishah* and *Derishah* commentaries on the *Arba'ah Turim*, as well as *Sefer Me'irat Enayim* on the *Code of Jewish Law*. Rabbi Falk was a pupil of Rabbi Moshe Isserles and served as head of the yeshivah in Lemberg, as well as on the Council of Four Lands, a central body of Jewish authority in Poland.

TEXT 1

Rabbi Yehoshua Falk, Perishah to the Tur, Yoreh Dei'ah 393:3

המקום ינחם אתכם בתוך שאר אבלי ציון וירושלים.

May the Omnipresent comfort you among the mourners of Zion and Jerusalem.

Question for Discussion

Rabbi Menachem Mendel Schneerson
1902–1994

The towering Jewish leader of the 20th century, known as "the Lubavitcher Rebbe," or simply as "the Rebbe." Born in southern Ukraine, the Rebbe escaped Nazi-occupied Europe, arriving in the U.S. in June 1941. The Rebbe inspired and guided the revival of traditional Judaism after the European devastation, impacting virtually every Jewish community the world over. The Rebbe often emphasized that the performance of just one additional good deed could usher in the era of Mashiach. The Rebbe's scholarly talks and writings have been printed in more than 200 volumes.

TEXT 2

The Lubavitcher Rebbe, Igrot Kodesh, vol. 25, pp. 3-5

ועוד נקודה ועיקר, נחמה בכפליים, אשר כמו שבודאי ובודאי יבנה
השם חרבות ציון וירושלים ויקבץ נדחי ישראל מכל קצוי תבל על
ידי משיח צדקנו ויביאם ברנה לראות בשמחתה של ציון וירושלים,
כך הוא ללא ספק בנוגע לאבל היחיד.

Another point and principle made by these words: Just as G-d will most certainly rebuild the ruins of Zion and Jerusalem and gather the dispersed of Israel from the ends of the earth through our righteous Moshiach, so will He, without a doubt, remove the grief of the individual.

The Nomadic Home

TEXT 3

Talmud Tractate Zevachim, 118b

תנו רבנן: ימי אהל מועד שבמדבר, ארבעים שנה חסר אחת. ימי
אהל מועד שבגלגל, ארבע עשרה, ז' שכבשו וז' שחלקו. ימי אהל
מועד שבנוב וגבעון, חמשים ושבע. נשתיירו לשילה ג' מאות
ושבעים חסר אחת.

Babylonian Talmud
A literary work of monumental proportions that draws upon the legal, spiritual, intellectual, ethical, and historical traditions of Judaism. The 37 tractates of the Babylonian Talmud contain the teachings of the Jewish sages from the period after the destruction of the 2nd Temple through the 5th century CE. It has served as the primary vehicle for the transmission of the Oral Law and the education of Jews over the centuries; it is the entry point for all subsequent legal, ethical, and theological Jewish scholarship.

Our rabbis taught: the duration of the Tent of Meeting in the wilderness was 39 years, the duration of the Tent of Meeting in Gilgal was 14 years—the 7 years of conquering and the 7 years of dividing the land—the duration of the Tent of Meeting in Nob and Gibeon combined was 57 years; there remains 369 years for the Tent of Meeting in Shiloh."

TEXT 4

Midrash Bereishit Rabah, 64:10

Bereishit Rabah

An early rabbinic commentary on the Book of Genesis. This Midrash bears the name of Rabbi Oshiya Rabah (Rabbi Oshiya "the Great") whose teaching opens this work. This Midrash provides textual exegeses and stories, expounds upon the biblical narrative, and develops and illustrates moral principles. Produced by the sages of the Talmud in the Land of Israel, its use of Aramaic closely resembles that of the Jerusalem Talmud. It was first printed in Constantinople in 1512 together with four other Midrashic works on the other four books of the Pentateuch.

בימי רבי יהושע בן חנניה גזרה מלכות הרשעה שיבנה בית המקדש. הושיבו פפוס ולוליאנוס טרפיזין מעכו עד אנטוכיא והיו מספקין לעולי גולה כסף וזהב וכל צרכם.

אזלין אלין כותאי ואמרין ידיע להוי למלכא דהדין קרתא מרדתא תתבנא ושוריא ישתכללון מנדה בלו והלך לא יתנון, מנדה, זו מדת הארץ, בלו, זו פרובגירון, והלך, זו אנגרוטינה, ואמר להון מה נעביד וגזרית, אמרין ליה שלח ואמר להון או ישנון יתיה מאתריה או יוספון עליה חמש אמין או יפצרון מיניה חמש אמין מן גרמיהון אנון חזרין בהון, והוון קהליא מצתין בהדא בקעתא דבית רמון כיון דאתון כתיבא שרון בכיין, בעיין לממרד על מלכותא אמרין יעול חד בר נש חכימא וישדך צבורא.

אמרין יעול רבי יהושע בן חנניה דהוא אסכולוסטקיא דאורייתא. עאל ודרש ארי טרף טרף ועמד עצם בגרונו אמר כל דאתי מפיק ליה אנא יהיב ליה אגריה. אתא הדין קורא מיצראה דמקוריה אריך יהיב מקוריה ואפקיה. אמר ליה הב לי אגרי! אמר ליה זיל תהא מלגלג ואומר דעילת לפומא דאריה בשלם ונפקת בשלם. כך דיינו שנכנסנו לאומה זו בשלום ויצאנו בשלום.

In the days of Rabbi Yehoshua ben Chananya, the Roman government decreed that the Temple be rebuilt. Two brothers, Pappos and Luliyanos, were appointed treasurers to oversee the funding of all the exiled Jews from Akko until Antioch.

But some Kutim went to the emperor and said, "The king should know that once Jerusalem is rebuilt and its walls fortified, the Jews will rebel against you and evade all taxes."

The emperor said, "What can I do> I have already decreed."

"Go and tell them," they responded, "that the Temple must be built in a different location than the Temple Mount, or that they must lengthen it by 5 cubits, or shorten it by 5 cubits. They will retract from the enterprise on their own accord."

The message was sent. When the Jews gathered in the field of Beit Rimon and saw the proclamation, they wept and galvanized themselves to rebel against the Empire.

The Sages, assured of this rebellion's bloody end, sought out Rabbi Yehoshua ben Chananya to placate the masses. He rose and said, "There was once a lion that devoured a beast. A bone, however, remained lodged in his throat. "Whoever can remove this bone will be rewarded," the lion said. There came a bird with a long beak who withdrew the bone from the lion's throat. "Where is my reward"? asked the bird. The lion said, "Go and proclaim the matter, that you escaped alive from the lion's mouth."

Yehoshua concluded, "Let it be enough that we entered into negotiations with the Empire and left unscathed." And the rebellion disbanded.

End of Optional Section

Don't Raise a Finger

G-d's Instructions

TEXT 5A

Yirmiyahu (Jeremiah) 25:9

הִנְנִי שֹׁלֵחַ וְלָקַחְתִּי אֶת כָּל מִשְׁפְּחוֹת צָפוֹן נְאֻם יְקֹוָק וְאֶל נְבוּכַדְרֶאצַּר מֶלֶךְ בָּבֶל עַבְדִּי וַהֲבִאֹתִים עַל הָאָרֶץ הַזֹּאת וְעַל יֹשְׁבֶיהָ וְעַל כָּל הַגּוֹיִם הָאֵלֶּה סָבִיב וְהַחֲרַמְתִּים וְשַׂמְתִּים לְשַׁמָּה וְלִשְׁרֵקָה וּלְחָרְבוֹת עוֹלָם:

"I am going to send for all the peoples of the north"—declares G-d—"and for My servant, King Nebuchadnezzar of Babylon, and bring them against this land and its inhabitants, and against all those nations roundabout. I will exterminate them and make them a desolation, an object of hissing—ruins for all time."

TEXT 5B

Ibid. 7:14

וְעָשִׂיתִי לַבַּיִת אֲשֶׁר נִקְרָא שְׁמִי עָלָיו אֲשֶׁר אַתֶּם בֹּטְחִים בּוֹ וְלַמָּקוֹם אֲשֶׁר נָתַתִּי לָכֶם וְלַאֲבוֹתֵיכֶם כַּאֲשֶׁר עָשִׂיתִי לְשִׁלוֹ:

"Therefore I will do *to the House that bears My name, on which you rely, and to the place that I gave you and your fathers, just what I did to Shiloh."*

Keeps His Own Commands

TEXT 6A

Tehillim (Psalms) 147:19

מַגִּיד דְּבָרָיו לְיַעֲקֹב חֻקָּיו וּמִשְׁפָּטָיו לְיִשְׂרָאֵל:

He tells His words to Jacob, His statutes and His ordinances to Israel.

TEXT 6B

Midrash Shemot Rabah, 30:9

Shemot Rabah

An early rabbinic commentary on the Book of Exodus. Midrash is the designation of a particular genre of rabbinic literature usually forming a running commentary on specific books of the Bible. *Shemot Rabah*, written mostly in Hebrew, provides textual exegeses, expounds upon the biblical narrative, and develops and illustrates moral principles. It was first printed in Constantinople in 1512 together with four other midrashic works on the other four books of the Pentateuch.

לפי שאין מדותיו של הקדוש ברוך הוא כמדת בשר ודם. מדת בשר
ודם מורה לאחרים לעשות והוא אינו עושה כלום. והקדוש ברוך הוא
אינו כן אלא מה שהוא עושה הוא אומר לישראל לעשות ולשמור.

[These words, statutes, and ordinances are called His because] G-d's ways are not like the ways of mortals. A mortal commands others to do, while he himself does nothing. G-d is not like that. Rather, He commands Israel to do and observe those things that He himself does.

Question—Do Not Waste

TEXT 7

Devarim (Deuteronomy) 20:19

כִּי תָצוּר אֶל עִיר יָמִים רַבִּים לְהִלָּחֵם עָלֶיהָ לְתָפְשָׂהּ לֹא תַשְׁחִית אֶת
עֵצָהּ לִנְדֹּחַ עָלָיו גַּרְזֶן כִּי מִמֶּנּוּ תֹאכֵל וְאֹתוֹ לֹא תִכְרֹת כִּי הָאָדָם עֵץ
הַשָּׂדֶה לָבֹא מִפָּנֶיךָ בַּמָּצוֹר:

When you besiege a city for many days to wage war against it to capture it, you shall not destroy its trees by wielding an ax against them, for you may eat from them, but you shall not cut them down. Is the tree of the field a man, to go into the siege before you?

TEXT 8A

Maimonides, Mishneh Torah, Laws of Kings and Wars, 6:10

Rabbi Moshe ben Maimon
(Maimonides, Rambam)
1135–1204
Halachist, philosopher, author, and physician. Maimonides was born in Cordoba, Spain. After the conquest of Cordoba by the Almohads, he fled Spain and eventually settled in Cairo, Egypt. There, he became the leader of the Jewish community and served as court physician to the vizier of Egypt. He is most noted for authoring the *Mishneh Torah*, an encyclopedic arrangement of Jewish law, and for his philosophical work, *Guide for the Perplexed*. His rulings on Jewish law are integral to the formation of halachic consensus.

ולא האילנות בלבד, אלא כל המשבר כלים, וקורע בגדים, והורס בנין, וסותם מעין, ומאבד מאכלות דרך השחתה, עובר בלא תשחית. ואינו לוקה אלא מכת מרדות מדבריהם.

This prohibition does not apply to trees alone. Rather, anyone who breaks utensils, tears garments, destroys buildings, stops up a spring, or ruins food with a destructive intent transgresses the command "Do not destroy."

Question—Do Not Destroy the Temple

TEXT 8B

Maimonides, Mishneh Torah, Laws of Beit Habechirah, 1:17

וכן הנותץ אבן אחת מן המזבח או מכל ההיכל או מבין האולם ולמזבח דרך השחתה לוקה שנאמר ונתצתם את מזבחותם וגו' לא תעשון כן לה' אלקיכם.

Anyone who demolishes a single stone from the Altar, any part of the Temple building, or [the floor of the Temple Courtyard] between the Entrance Hall and the Altar with a destructive intent is worthy of lashes, as the verse states, "And you shall destroy their altars.... Do not do so to G-d, your G-d."

A Hopeful Hammer
"Not for the Sake of Demolition"

TEXT 9

Rabbi Moshe Isserles (Rema)
1525–1572
Halachist. Rama served as rabbi in Krakow, Poland, and is considered the definitive authority on Jewish law among Ashkenazic Jewry. Rama authored glosses on the Shulchan Aruch (known as the *Mapah*) and *Darchei Moshe*, a commentary on the halachic compendium *Arba'ah Turim*.

Rabbi Moshe Isserles, Glosses of Rema to Shulchan Aruch, Orach Chaim, 152:1

ואסור לסתור דבר מבית הכנסת, אלא אם כן עושה על מנת לבנות.

It is forbidden to destroy any part of a synagogue, unless it is in order to build.

TEXT 10

Midrash Yalkut Shimoni, Yirmiyahu §259

Yalkut Shimoni
A Midrash that covers the entire Biblical text. Its material is collected from all over rabbinic literature, including the Babylonian and Jerusalem Talmuds and various ancient Midrashic texts. It contains several passages from Midrashim that have been lost, as well as different versions of existing Midrashim. It is unclear when and by whom this Midrash was redacted.

עלה אריה במזל אריה והחריב את אריאל. עלה אריה - זה נבוכדנאצר, דכתיב: עלה אריה מסבכו. במזל אריה - עד גלות ירושלים בחדש החמישי. והחריב אריאל - הוי אריאל אריאל קרית חנה דוד. על מנת שיבא אריה במזל אריה ויבנה אריאל. יבא אריה - זה הקב"ה, דכתיב ביה: אריה שאג מי לא יירא. במזל אריה - והפכתי אבלם לששון. ויבנה אריאל - בונה ירושלים ה' נדחי ישראל יכנס.

A Lion rose in the constellation of the lion and destroyed the lion. A lion rose—this refers to Nebuchadnezzar, as it is written, "The lion has come up from his thicket." In the constellation of the lion, as it is written,

"...Jerusalem went into exile in the fifth month" [the month of Av whose constellation is the lion]. And destroyed the lion—this is the Temple, as it is written, "Ah, Lion, Lion, city where David camped!"

All this was on condition that the lion will come in the constellation of the lion and rebuild the lion. The lion will come, this refers to G-d, as it is written, "A lion has roared, who can but fear? My Lord G-d has spoken, who can but prophesize?" In the constellation of the lion, as it is written, "I will turn their mourning to joy" [so that the same month of Av that was once a mournful one will then be joyous]. And rebuild the lion, as it is written, "G-d rebuilds Jerusalem. He gathers the exiles of Israel."

A Two-Faced Prophecy

TEXT 11

Michah, 3:12

לָכֵן בִּגְלַלְכֶם צִיּוֹן שָׂדֶה תֵחָרֵשׁ וִירוּשָׁלַם עִיּין תִּהְיֶה וְהַר הַבַּיִת לְבָמוֹת יָעַר:

Therefore, because of you, Zion shall be plowed as a field; Jerusalem shall become heaps, and the Temple Mount like the high places of a forest.

Question for discussion:

TEXT 12

Rabbi Shmuel Eidel's, Maharsha, Chidushei Agadot, Shabbat, 139a

Rabbi Shmuel Eliezer Halevi Eidel's
(Maharsha)
1555–1632

Rabbi, author, and Talmudist. Rabbi Eidel's established a yeshivah in Posen, Poland, which was supported by his mother-in-law, Eidel (hence his surname is "Eidel's"). He is primarily known for his *Chidushei Halachot*, a commentary on the Talmud in which he resolves difficulties in the texts of the Talmud, Rashi, and *Tosafot*, and which is a basic work for those who seek an in-depth understanding of the Talmud; and for his *Chidushei Agadot*, his innovative commentary on the homiletic passages of the Talmud.

לא בכליון גמור כמו בסדום דהיינו ציון שדה תחרש ויהיה ראוי
לזריעה.

This prophecy intimates that the destruction is not complete… for "Zion shall be plowed as a field" means like a field that is ready to be sowed."

A Place to Rest Forever

TEXT 13

Zohar, vol. 3, 121b

דכד נפקו ישראל ממצרים בעא קב"ה למעבד לון בארעא כמלאכין
קדישין לעילא ובעא למבני לון ביתא קדישא ולנחתא ליה מגו שמי
רקיעין ולנטעא לון לישראל נציבא קדישא כגוונא דדיוקנא דלעילא.
הה"ד תביאמו ותטעמו בהר נחלתך. באן אתר במכון לשבתך פעלת
ה' בההוא דפעלת אנת ה' ולא אחרא. מכון לשבתך פעלתך ה' דא
בית ראשון. מקדש ה' כוננו ידיך דא בית שני ותרוייהו אומנותא
דקב"ה אינון.

ומדארגיזו קמיה במדברא מיתו ואכנס לון קב"ה לבנייהו בארעא
(אליפו עובדיהון) וביתא אתבני על ידא דבר נש. ובגין כך לא
אתקיים. ושלמה הוה ידע דבגין דאי עובדא דבר נש לא יתקיים
ועל דא אמר אם ה' לא יבנה בית שוא עמלו בוניו בו דהא לית ליה
ביה קיומא. ביומוי דעזרא גרם חטאה ואצטרכון אינון למבני ולא
הוה ביה קיומא.

ועד כען בניינא קדמאה דקב"ה לא הוה בעלמא ולזמנא דאתי כתיב
בונה ירושלם ה' איהו ולא אחרא. ובניינא דא אנן מחכאן ולא בניינא
דבר נש דלית ביה קיומא כלל.

Zohar
The seminal work of Kabbalah, Jewish mysticism. The Zohar is a mystical commentary on the Torah, written in Aramaic and Hebrew. According to Arizal, the Zohar contains the teachings of Rabbi Shimon bar Yocha'i who lived in the Land of Israel during the second century. The Zohar has become one of the indispensable texts of traditional Judaism, alongside and nearly equal in stature to the Mishnah and Talmud.

When Israel left Egypt, G-d desired to install them in the land like celestial angels, and to build for them a holy house, to bring it down from Heaven, and to plant Israel in the earth as a holy seedling, just like their ideal, Heavenly form.

As it says, "You will bring them and plant them in Your own mountain." In what place? The verse continues, "The place You made to dwell in, O Lord"; this means in the place that You, G-d, create, and in no other…

But when Israel angered G-d in the desert, they died. And G-d brought their children into the land, and the Temple was built by human hands. Therefore, it did not last. King Solomon knew that the work of mortals cannot last; thus he said, "Unless the Lord builds the house, its builders labor in vain…." In vain because it will not last. Then, in the days of Ezra, when they built the Second Temple, they sinned again. And so that did not last either.

Thus, until today, G-d's original home has not yet entered the world. Regarding the future, it is said, "G-d builds Jerusalem." He will build it, and no other.

It is for this building that we wait, not for any man-made structure that cannot last forever.

Dare We Hope?

TEXT 14

Rabbi Yisrael Baal Shem Tov, Keter Shem Tov, *§237*

דרך משל אדם שיש לו בן קטן ורוצה להרגיל אותו לילך, מעמידו
על הארץ, ומתרחק ממנו מעט, וקוראהו שילך הקטן אצלו מעט,
וכאשר בא התינוק אל אביו אז מתרחק אביו עוד ממנו, והולך
התינוק עוד אצלו, ועושה האב כזה כמה וכמה פעמים עד שמרגילו
לבא להליכה גמורה.

ונבין מזה המשל כי כל מה שמתרחק האב מן התינוק תמיד, הוא
כדי שילך התינוק עוד להלן, מה שאין כן אם לא היה האב מתרחק
מהתינוק כשבא אצלו בפעם ראשונה, הוה התינוק עומד ונשאר
במקום ההוא הראשון ולא היה הולך להלך עוד.

Rabbi Yisrael Baal Shem Tov (Besht)
1698–1760
Founder of the Chasidic movement. Born in Slutsk, Belarus, the Baal Shem Tov was orphaned as a child. He served as a teacher's assistant and clay digger before founding the Chasidic movement and revolutionizing the Jewish world with his emphasis on prayer, joy, and love for every Jew, regardless of his or her level of Torah knowledge.

How does a parent teach a child to walk? By placing the child on the floor, at a distance, and encouraging him to come closer. The child will approach, wobbling on his frail feet. Yet the nearer the child comes, the farther the parent retreats. So it goes, over and over, nearer then farther, nearer then farther, until the child learns to walk on his own.

We can understand in the analogy, the great distance between the parent and the child is to teach the child to walk further. Contrarily, if the parent would not retreat from the child the first time he or she approached, the child would stay in the same place forever.

TEXT 15

Kohelet (Ecclesiastes) 3:1–4

לַכֹּל זְמָן וְעֵת לְכָל חֵפֶץ תַּחַת הַשָּׁמָיִם:
עֵת לָלֶדֶת וְעֵת לָמוּת עֵת לָטַעַת וְעֵת לַעֲקוֹר נָטוּעַ:
עֵת לַהֲרוֹג וְעֵת לִרְפּוֹא עֵת לִפְרוֹץ וְעֵת לִבְנוֹת:
עֵת לִבְכּוֹת וְעֵת לִשְׂחוֹק עֵת סְפוֹד וְעֵת רְקוֹד:

Everything has an appointed season, and there is a time for every matter under the heaven.

A time to give birth and a time to die; a time to plant and a time to uproot that which is planted.

A time to kill and a time to heal; a time to break and a time to build.

A time to weep and a time to laugh; a time of wailing and a time of dancing.

3

VA'ETCHANAN

Summoning the Love

How to Master the Emotional Roadmap

Dedicated in honor of the birthday of our friend **Rabbi Sholom Ber Lipskar**, 4 Menachem Av.
May he and his family merit to witness the fulfillment of continuous blessings
for health, happiness, nachas and success in all their endeavors.

PARASHAH OVERVIEW
Va'Etchanan

Moses tells the people of Israel how he implored *G-d to allow him to enter the Land of Israel, but G-d refused, instructing him instead to ascend a mountain and* see the Promised Land.

Continuing his "review of the Torah," Moses describes the Exodus from Egypt and the Giving of the Torah, declaring them unprecedented events *in human history. "Has there ever occurred this great thing, or has the likes of it ever been heard? Did ever a people hear the voice of G-d speaking out of the midst of the fire . . . and live? . . . You were shown, to know, that the L-rd is G-d . . .* there is none else beside Him."

Moses predicts that in future generations the people will turn away from G-d, worship idols, and be exiled *from their land and scattered amongst the nations; but* from there *they will seek G-d, and* return *to obey His commandments.*

Our Parshah also includes a repetition of the Ten Commandments, *and the verses of the Shema, which declare the fundamentals of the Jewish faith: the* unity of G-d *("Hear O Israel: the L-rd our G-d, the L-rd is one"); the* mitzvot *to* love *G-d, to* study *His Torah, and to bind "these words" as* tefillin *on our arms and heads, and inscribe them in the* mezuzot *affixed on the doorposts of our homes.*

A Puzzling Command

Love: A Paradox?

TEXT 1

Rabbi Shalom Dovber of Lubavitch, Sefer Hama'amarim 5666, p.577

Rabbi Shalom Dovber Schneersohn
(Rashab)
1860– 1920
Chasidic rebbe. Rabbi Shalom Dovber became the fifth leader of the Chabad movement upon the passing of his father, Rabbi Shmuel of Lubavitch. He established the Lubavitch network of *yeshivot* called Tomchei Temimim. He authored many volumes of chasidic discourses and is renowned for his lucid and thorough explanations of kabbalistic concepts.

אך הנה מורגל בלשון העולם דאהבה שהוא אוהב לזולתו שזהו מה
שאוהב את עצמו, דאס איז וואס ער האט זיך האלט, והאמת הוא
כן דאהבה היא חוזרת אל האוהב, הרי מזה מובן דמה שהוא אוהב
אל הזולת, הוא אהבת עצמו, ובאמת האהבה היא חוזרת כו'... וכמו
שאנו רואים באהבת הבנים שזהו מפני שהם שייכים אליו שהרי
לבנים אחרים אין לו אהבה מפני שאינם שייכים אליו ורק לבניו
שהם שייכים אליו שם היא האהבה בתוקף והתגלות ואם כן זה
אהבת עצמו.

It is commonly said that loving another is loving oneself, and this is true, since love reflects back upon the lover. The notion that a person "loves another individual" is in reality "self-love," since love by its nature reflects. For example, a father loves his sons because they are related to him. Another person's son he does not love, because they are not related. Only toward his own son does he feel a strong and revealed love. If so, this is self-love.

The Mitzvah to Love G-d

TEXT 2

Devarim (Deuteronomy) 6:4-9

שְׁמַע יִשְׂרָאֵל ה' אֱלֹקֵינוּ ה' אֶחָד:

וְאָהַבְתָּ אֵת ה' אֱלֹקֶיךָ בְּכָל לְבָבְךָ וּבְכָל נַפְשְׁךָ וּבְכָל מְאֹדֶךָ:

וְהָיוּ הַדְּבָרִים הָאֵלֶּה אֲשֶׁר אָנֹכִי מְצַוְּךָ הַיּוֹם עַל לְבָבֶךָ:

וְשִׁנַּנְתָּם לְבָנֶיךָ וְדִבַּרְתָּ בָּם בְּשִׁבְתְּךָ בְּבֵיתֶךָ וּבְלֶכְתְּךָ בַדֶּרֶךְ וּבְשָׁכְבְּךָ וּבְקוּמֶךָ:

וּקְשַׁרְתָּם לְאוֹת עַל יָדֶךָ וְהָיוּ לְטֹטָפֹת בֵּין עֵינֶיךָ:

וּכְתַבְתָּם עַל מְזֻזֹת בֵּיתֶךָ וּבִשְׁעָרֶיךָ:

Hear, O Israel: The Lord is our G-d; the Lord is one.

And you shall love the Lord, your G-d, with all your heart and with all your soul, and with all your means.

And these words, which I command you this day, shall be upon your heart.

And you shall teach them to your sons and speak of them when you sit in your house, and when you walk on the way, and when you lie down and when you rise up.

And you shall bind them for a sign upon your hand, and they shall be for ornaments between your eyes.

And you shall inscribe them upon the doorposts of your house and upon your gates.

Rabbi Moshe ben Maimon (Maimonides, Rambam)
1135–1204

Halachist, philosopher, author, and physician. Maimonides was born in Cordoba, Spain. After the conquest of Cordoba by the Almohads, he fled Spain and eventually settled in Cairo, Egypt. There, he became the leader of the Jewish community and served as court physician to the vizier of Egypt. He is most noted for authoring the *Mishneh Torah*, an encyclopedic arrangement of Jewish law, and for his philosophical work, *Guide for the Perplexed*. His rulings on Jewish law are integral to the formation of halachic consensus.

TEXT 3

Maimonides, Sefer Hamitzvot, Positive Mitzvah 3

המצווה השלישית היא הציווי שנצטווינו על אהבתו יתעלה.

The third mitzvah is the commandment to love G-d, the exalted One.

TEXT 4

Rabbi Shneur Zalman of Liadi, Tanya, ch. 4

האהבה היא שורש כל רמ"ח מצוות עשה, וממנה הן נמשכות,
ובלעדה אין להן קיום אמיתי. כי המקיימן באמת, הוא האוהב את
שם ה' וחפץ לדבקה בו באמת, ואי אפשר לדבקה בו באמת כי
אם בקיום רמ"ח פקודין שהם רמ"ח אברין דמלכא כביכול, כמו
שבארנו במקום אחר.

*Love of G-d is the root of all 248 positive command-
ments, and they flow from it. Without love of G-d,
those commandments are not truly fulfilled. Only one
who loves G-d and truly desires to cleave to Him really
fulfills these commandments, since it is impossible to
cleave to G-d except through the fulfillment of these
248 commandments, since they are like the 248 limbs
and organs of the King, as is explained elsewhere.*

**Rabbi Shneur
Zalman of Liadi**
(Alter Rebbe)
1745–1812
Chasidic rebbe, halachic
authority, and founder of
the Chabad movement. The
Alter Rebbe was born in
Liozna, Belarus, and was
among the principal students
of the Magid of Mezeritch.
His numerous works include
the *Tanya*, an early classic
containing the fundamentals
of Chabad Chasidism, and
Shulchan Aruch HaRav,
an expanded and reworked
code of Jewish law.

A Second Facet

TEXT 5

Devarim (Deuteronomy), 11:13-21

וְהָיָה אִם שָׁמֹעַ תִּשְׁמְעוּ אֶל מִצְוֹתַי אֲשֶׁר אָנֹכִי מְצַוֶּה אֶתְכֶם הַיּוֹם לְאַהֲבָה אֶת ה' אֱלֹקֵיכֶם וּלְעָבְדוֹ בְּכָל לְבַבְכֶם וּבְכָל נַפְשְׁכֶם:

וְנָתַתִּי מְטַר אַרְצְכֶם בְּעִתּוֹ יוֹרֶה וּמַלְקוֹשׁ וְאָסַפְתָּ דְגָנֶךָ וְתִירֹשְׁךָ וְיִצְהָרֶךָ:

וְנָתַתִּי עֵשֶׂב בְּשָׂדְךָ לִבְהֶמְתֶּךָ וְאָכַלְתָּ וְשָׂבָעְתָּ:

הִשָּׁמְרוּ לָכֶם פֶּן יִפְתֶּה לְבַבְכֶם וְסַרְתֶּם וַעֲבַדְתֶּם אֱלֹהִים אֲחֵרִים וְהִשְׁתַּחֲוִיתֶם לָהֶם:

וְחָרָה אַף ה' בָּכֶם וְעָצַר אֶת הַשָּׁמַיִם וְלֹא יִהְיֶה מָטָר וְהָאֲדָמָה לֹא תִתֵּן אֶת יְבוּלָהּ וַאֲבַדְתֶּם מְהֵרָה מֵעַל הָאָרֶץ הַטֹּבָה אֲשֶׁר ה' נֹתֵן לָכֶם:

וְשַׂמְתֶּם אֶת דְּבָרַי אֵלֶּה עַל לְבַבְכֶם וְעַל נַפְשְׁכֶם וּקְשַׁרְתֶּם אֹתָם לְאוֹת עַל יֶדְכֶם וְהָיוּ לְטוֹטָפֹת בֵּין עֵינֵיכֶם:

וְלִמַּדְתֶּם אֹתָם אֶת בְּנֵיכֶם לְדַבֵּר בָּם בְּשִׁבְתְּךָ בְּבֵיתֶךָ וּבְלֶכְתְּךָ בַדֶּרֶךְ וּבְשָׁכְבְּךָ וּבְקוּמֶךָ:

וּכְתַבְתָּם עַל מְזוּזוֹת בֵּיתֶךָ וּבִשְׁעָרֶיךָ:

לְמַעַן יִרְבּוּ יְמֵיכֶם וִימֵי בְנֵיכֶם עַל הָאֲדָמָה אֲשֶׁר נִשְׁבַּע ה' לַאֲבֹתֵיכֶם לָתֵת לָהֶם כִּימֵי הַשָּׁמַיִם עַל הָאָרֶץ:

And it will be, if you listen to My commandments I command you this day to love the Lord, your G-d, and to serve Him with all your heart and with all your soul.

I will give the rain of your land at its time, the early rain and the latter rain, and you will gather in your grain, your wine, and your oil.

And I will give grass in your field for your livestock, and you will eat and be sated.

Beware, lest your heart be misled, and you turn away and worship strange gods and prostrate yourselves before them.

And the wrath of G-d will be kindled against you, and He will close off the heavens, and there will be no rain, and the ground will not give its produce, and you will perish quickly from upon the good land that G-d gives you.

And you shall set these words of Mine upon your heart and upon your soul, and bind them for a sign upon your hand and they shall be for ornaments between your eyes.

And you shall teach them to your sons to speak with them, when you sit in your house and when you walk on the way and when you lie down and when you rise.

And you shall inscribe them upon the doorposts of your house and upon your gates, in order that your days may increase and the days of your children, on the land that G-d swore to your forefathers to give them, as the days of heaven above the earth.

Love and Nothingness

Independence vs. Nullification

TEXT 6A

Rabbi Shneur Zalman of Liadi, Tanya, ch. 22

> עיקר ושרש עבודה זרה הוא מה שנחשב לדבר בפני עצמו נפרד
> מקדושתו של מקום ולא כפירה בה׳ לגמרי.

The main thrust and core notion of idol worship is not outright denial of G-d, but merely that something is considered an independent being, separate from G-d's holiness.

TEXT 6B

Tanya, ch. 6

> וצד הקדושה אינו אלא השראה והמשכה מקדושתו של הקדוש
> ברוך הוא ואין הקדוש ברוך הוא שורה אלא על דבר שבטל אצלו
> יתברך בין בפועל ממש כמלאכים עליונים בין בכח ככל איש ישראל
> למטה שבכחו להיות בטל ממש לגבי הקדוש ברוך הוא.

Holiness is simply the presence and influence of G-d's sanctity. G-d only dwells in a place that is nullified to him. This nullification can be both actual, like that of the supernal angels, or in potential, like the ability of every Jew to become literally nullified to G-d.

The Process of Nullification

TEXT 7

Tanya, ch. 1-2

דלכל איש ישראל אחד צדיק ואחד רשע יש שתי נשמות דכתיב
"ונשמות אני עשיתי" שהן שתי נפשות נפש אחת מצד הקליפה
וסטרא אחרא והיא המתלבשת בדם האדם להחיות הגוף.
ונפש השנית בישראל היא חלק אלוק ממעל ממש.

Every Jew, whether righteous or wicked, has two souls, as it is written, "And I have created souls" [plural]. One of these two souls comes from the concealment of G-d and the "other side," and it is invested in one's blood to give life to the body.

But the second soul of a Jew is a part of G-d above, literally.

TEXT 8

Rabbi Shneur Zalman of Liadi, Shulchan Aruch HaRav,
Orach Chaim Mahadura Batra 4:2

שגמר ועיקר כניסת נפש הקדושה באדם הוא בי״ג שנים ויום א׳
לזכר וי״ב לנקבה... ותחלת כניסת נפש זו הקדושה היא בחינוך
לתורה ולמצות שחייבו חכמים לחנך (ו)גם במצות מילה.

The conclusion of the process of the holy soul entering the person, indeed, the primary step of that process, takes place when a male reaches thirteen years and one day, or for a female, twelve years and a day. The process begins at the beginning of education in Torah and mitzvot (as the obligation of the parents by rabbinic decree) and also at the performance of the circumcision.

Rabbi Menachem Mendel Schneersohn of Lubavitch
(*Tzemach Tzedek*)
1789–1866

Chasidic rebbe and noted author. The *Tzemach Tzedek* was the third leader of the Chabad Chasidic movement and a noted authority on Jewish law. His numerous works include halachic responsa, Chasidic discourses, and Kabbalistic writings. Active in the plight of Russian Jewry, he worked to alleviate the plight of the Cantonists, Jewish children kidnapped to serve in the Czar's army. He passed away in Lubavitch, leaving seven sons and two daughters.

What Love Is

TEXT 9

Rabbi Menachem Mendel Schneersohn of Lubavitch, the Tzemach
Tzedek, Derech Mitzvotecha, Mitzvat Achdut Hashem, Chapter 3

שעל פי האמת אין הנבראים בחינת יש ודבר כמו שנראים אנחנו
בעינינו.. ונמצא שאין עוד שום מציאות כלל זולת מציאותו ית׳ והרי
זה היחוד הגמור. ולכן צריך להיות בחינת אין ואפס וכמותר בעולם
ולא לומר אני אלא לעשות מאני אין (עש איז ניטא קיין אין).

In reality, creation is not a yesh or an independent entity as it appears… There is no existence at all aside from His blessed existence; everything exists in complete unity with the Creator. Therefore, we must view ourselves as superfluous non-entities, and should not call ourselves "I" but rather "nothing."

"All Your Hearts"

TEXT 10

The Lubavitcher Rebbe, Sefer Hama'amarim Melukat, vol. 2 p. 40

האהבה דבכל לבבך היא מצד ההבנה וההשגה (שאלקות הוא טוב).

The love of "with all your hearts" derives from the understanding that G-dliness is good.

Rabbi Menachem Mendel Schneerson
1902–1994

The towering Jewish leader of the 20th century, known as "the Lubavitcher Rebbe," or simply as "the Rebbe." Born in southern Ukraine, the Rebbe escaped Nazi-occupied Europe, arriving in the U.S. in June 1941. The Rebbe inspired and guided the revival of traditional Judaism after the European devastation, impacting virtually every Jewish community the world over. The Rebbe often emphasized that the performance of just one additional good deed could usher in the era of Mashiach. The Rebbe's scholarly talks and writings have been printed in more than 200 volumes.

TEXT 11

Derech Mitzvotecha, Shoresh Mitzvat Hatefillah, ch. 42

והנה פירוש בכל לבבך בשני יצריך שגם היצר הרע והנפש השכלית
ישוב לאהבת ה׳ מחמת ההתבוננות הנ״ל שגם השכל יסכים על זה.

The reason why the verse says "with all your hearts" (in the plural) is because it refers to both inclinations, the tendency to good and to evil. [At this level of love], even the evil inclination and the rational soul can come to love G-d through the power of rational argument.

"With All Your Soul"

TEXT 12

The Lubavitcher Rebbe, Sefer HaMa'amarim Melukat, vol. 4 p. 203

והענין הוא, דפירוש בכל נפשך הוא בכל כחות הנפש, שכל ומדות.
ויש לומר הכוונה בזה, שמעלת האהבה דבכל נפשך על האהבה
דבכל לבבך היא, שבהאהבה דבכל לבבך העיקר היא המדה [שלכן
נאמר בה בכל לבבך דלב הוא מקום משכן המדות], כי ההשגה
שמולידה אהבה זו היא בחיצוניות השכל השייך למדות, וההשגה
דבחינה זו היא במוח ואינה מאירה בלב, ולכן הולדת האהבה
מהשכל אינה בדרך ממילא אלא שהשכל צריך לפעול את האהבה.
ובהאהבה דבכל נפשך, ההשגה שממנה באה האהבה היא בפנימיות
השכל, שההשגה דבחינה זו מאירה בלב, והמשכת האהבה מהשכל
היא באופן דבדרך ממילא. ולכן נאמר בה בכל נפשך, כל כחות
הנפש, כי באהבה זו נרגש גם השכל....
ועוד ביאור בהחילוק שבין האהבה דבכל לבבך והאהבה דבכל
נפשך, שהאהבה דבכל לבבך היא בבחינת ממלא כל עלמין, דכיון
שהחיות דבחינת ממכ"ע הוא מלובש בהנבראים בפנימיותם, לכן
על ידי ההתבוננות נרגש חיות זה גם בנפש הבהמית, והאהבה היא
בכל לבבך בשני יצריך.
והאהבה דבכל נפשך היא בבחינת סוכ"ע, דכיון שאור הסובב הוא
למעלה מהתלבשות בעולמות, לכן על ידי שנרגש בו ההפלאה
דאור אין סוף (סובב), אהבתו את הוי' היא באופן דמסירת נפש,
אפילו נוטל את נפשך.

*"With all your soul" means "with all the faculties" of
the soul—intellectual and emotional.*

The advantage of love "with all your soul" over love "with all your hearts" is that the latter is centered on the emotion [which is why it refers to the heart]. This is because the love "with all your hearts" is the outcome of only superficial thinking, which aims to move the heart and therefore must cater to the needs of the emotions.

[Love] "with all your soul," however, is an expression of true intellect, which affects the emotions automatically rather than by catering to their needs. This is why it is called "with all your soul," with all the faculties of the soul, because "objective" intellect is involved in this love, beyond the emotions and their needs…

Another explanation of the difference between love "with all your hearts" and love "with all your soul:" Love "with all your hearts" derives from contemplating the immanence of G-d within the world. Since G-d's immanence comprises the very identity of creation, through contemplating it one can "feel the G-dliness" even within the Animal Soul, and can love G-d with "all your hearts," in the plural – with both the positive and negative inclination.

Love "with all your soul," however, is not fueled by G-d's immanence but by His transcendence. At that level, G-d is far above investment within the worlds, so by contemplating this, one feels more of G-d's aloofness and marvel. The resultant love is the love of self-sacrifice; the person is literally prepared to give "all your soul" for G-d.

TEXT 13A

Rabbi Yosef Yitzchak Schneersohn of Lubavitch,
Sefer Hama'amarim Kuntresim 2, p. 351

האהבה דבכל נפשך היא הגדלת האהבה שהאהבה מתפשטת גם בשארי כחות ואיברים, כמו המדבר דברי תורה מזה שהוא בקי בעל פה בכל עת שהוא פנוי מלמוד עיוני,או בבעל עסק שבעת שהוא פנוי מעסקו, או הרץ לדבר מצוה, והמתעסק בהרבצת התורה בגופו וטרחתו, שכל זה הוא מפני יוקר המצות וחיבתן... וסיבת היוקר היא מפני אהבת ה'.

Love "with all your soul" is a growing love, a love that extends to all faculties and organs. This love is what causes a person to use his free time from in-depth study to speak words of Torah by heart. This loves causes a worker to learn when he is free from work; it makes one rush to perform a mitzvah, or to work with physical exertion and strain to strengthen the Torah. All of this is because he cherishes the mitzvot... *The reason why one would cherish a mitzvah is because he loves G-d.*

Rabbi Yosef Yitzchak Schneersohn
(Rayatz, Frierdiker Rebbe, Previous Rebbe)
1880–1950

Chasidic rebbe, prolific writer, and Jewish activist. Rabbi Yosef Yitzchak, the 6th leader of the Chabad movement, actively promoted Jewish religious practice in Soviet Russia and was arrested for these activities. After his release from prison and exile, he settled in Warsaw, Poland, from where he fled Nazi occupation, and arrived in New York in 1940. Settling in Brooklyn, Rabbi Schneersohn worked to revitalize American Jewish life. His son-in law, Rabbi Menachem Mendel Schneerson, succeeded him as the leader of the Chabad movement.

TEXT 13B

Rabbi Yosef Yitzchak Schneerson of Lubavitch,
Sefer Hama'amarim 5666 p. 497

דבכל נפשך הוא כאשר האהבה מתגברת יותר עד שפועלת גם
באברים החיצונים וכמו הרץ לדבר מצוה וכה"ג וכמו על דרך
משל אמת המים שעל ידי ריבוי גשמים או הפשרת שלגים ה"ה
מתפשטת על גדותיה כו', וכמו כן כאשר תתגבר האהבה בלב יותר
הרי היא מתפשטת גם באברים החיצונים.

"With all your soul" is when the love is so strong that if affects even the external limbs, such as one who runs to perform a mitzvah or the like. Like water from excessive rain or the melting snow extending to fill irrigation canals, this love is so powerful that it "overflows" the heart and extends to the external limbs.

"With All Your Means"

TEXT 14A

The Lubavitcher Rebbe, Sefer Hama'amarim Melukat, vol. 2, p. 41.

האהבה דבכל מאדך הוא ענין המסירת נפש.
דלכאורה אינו מובן, והרי גם האהבה בכל לבבך ובכל נפשך מחייבת
לכאורה ענין המסירת נפש, דכשאוהב את הוי' בכל לבבו ועל אחת
כמה וכמה כשאהבתו את הוי' היא בכל נפשו הרי בודאי ימסור
נפשו עבורו, ומהו העילוי והחידוש בהאהבה דבכל מאדך?
והביאור בזה, שהמסירת נפש שמצד האהבה דבכל לבבך ובכל
נפשך היא באופן שרוצה למסור נפשו עבור הוי'... מה שאין כן
המסירת נפש שמצד האהבה דבכל מאדך, יחידה, היא באופן שאינו
יכול להיות נפרד ח"ו. וזהו שענין המסירת נפש הוא בהאהבה דבכל
מאדך, כי מסירת נפש הוא ענין הביטול, ואמיתית ענין הביטול הוא
כשהמסירת נפש היא לא מצד הרצון (מציאות) של.

Love "with all your means" is the love of self-sacrifice.

What does that mean? Don't the other forms of love also require self-sacrifice? Both the love "with all your hearts" and certainly the love "with all your soul" will bring a person to sacrifice their life for G-d, so what is the unique quality of the love "with all your means"?

The explanation: Self-sacrifice that flows from the other types of love is born of a desire to give one's life for G-d. Love "with all your means," however, is not a form of self-sacrifice that a person desires, but rather the simple inability to separate from G-d, Heaven forbid. This self-sacrifice is the true bittul, *inasmuch that the person does not even desire it (desire being indicative of a unique existence).*

TEXT 14B

Ibid.

שזהו ההפרש בין המסירת נפש דאברהם אבינו להמסירת נפש
דרבי עקיבא, דהמסירת נפש דרבי עקיבא היה וואָס ער האָט געזוכט
מסירת נפש, מתי יבוא לידי ואקיימנו, מה שאין כן באברהם הנה
המסירת נפש שלו היה בדרך אגב. דאברהם ידע שעיקר העבודה
הוא כמו שכתוב ויקרא שם בשם הוי׳ אל עולם, אל תקרי ויקרא
אלא ויקריא, אַז יענער זאָל אויך שרייען, ואם נצרך לזה בדרך אגב
מסירת נפש, הנה גם זה ישנו.

This, then, is the difference between the self-sacrifice of Abraham and that of Rabbi Akiva. Rabbi Akiva sought out self-sacrifice, and wondered, "When it will come my way so that I may fulfill it," whereas the self-sacrifice of Abraham was incidental. That is, Abraham knew that his primary Divine mission was to spread G-dly awareness throughout the world; if it so happened that this mission would require giving his life, he was ready to do that too.

Above and Within

The One and the Many

TEXT 15

Rabbi Tzadok Hakohen of Lublin, Tzidkat HaTzaddik, Section 224

כל אדם צריך לקבל עליו עול מלכות שמים בכל יום בתכלית התוקף שמתרצה למסור עצמו לגמרי ולהכלל במקורו. וזהו פרשה ראשונה דקריאת שמע הגם דפרשה שניה אחר כך נאמר ואספת דגנך שלמדו מזה בברכות הנהג בהן מנהג דרך ארץ (לחרוש בשעת חרישה וכו') שהיא בלשון רבים אמורה.

ואמרינן שם הרבה עשו כר' שמעון בר יוחאי ולא עלתה בידם דאי אפשר לרבים ולכל העולם כולו להיות כר' שמעון בר יוחאי ולכך לא נאמר שם בכל מאדך שפירוש ממונך להפקיר הכל שזה אינו לרבים שצריכים לנהוג במדת דרך ארץ ולהשגיח על ממונם גם כן להיות במה להתפרנס וקיום חיותם...

מה שאין כן פרשה ראשונה דנאמר בלשון יחיד ליחידים אשר ה' קורא כרבי שמעון בר יוחאי נאמר בכל מאדך היינו להיות מופקר לגמרי...

וכל אחד צריך גם כן לומר פרשה ראשונה גם כן שתחלת קבלתו בכל יום עול מלכות שמים צריך להיות בענין זה גם להיות מופקר אם יהיה רצון הש"י כן...

וכן אפילו אותם היחידים צריכים גם כן שיאמרו פרשת והיה אם שמוע כמו שאמרו לר' שמעון בר יוחאי בשבת שיחזור למערה כי אי אפשר להיות כן רק במערה וחוץ לעולם אבל בעולם הזה הקדוש ברוך הוא רוצה בישוב

Rabbi Tzadok Hakohen Rabinowitz of Lublin
1823–1900
Chasidic master and thinker. Rabbi Tzadok was born into a Lithuanian rabbinic family and later joined the Chasidic movement. He was a follower of the Chasidic leaders Rabbi Mordechai Yosef Leiner of Izbica and Rabbi Leibel Eiger. He succeeded Rabbi Eiger after his passing and became a rebbe in Lublin, Poland. He authored many works on Jewish law, Chasidism, Kabbalah, and ethics, as well as scholarly essays on astronomy, geometry, and algebra.

העולם ולא תוהו בראה וגו' והנהגה זו לצאת מגבולו ומכפי מה
שהוא כלי לקבל בעודו בגוף זהו הנהגה מעולם התוהו.

*Every person must accept the yoke of G-d's kingship
upon themselves daily to the utmost, wishing to be completely devoted to G-d and be consumed within Him.
This is expressed in the first paragraph of the Shema.*

*By contrast, the second paragraph says, "And you will
gather in your grain." From this the Talmud learns
that "we are to cultivate the land" (plow at the appropriate time, etc.). The language is in the plural form,
implying that the entire Jewish people will work the
land, etc.*

*Now, the Talmud explains that many tried to act like
Rabbi Shimon Bar Yochai. His philosophy was that
if one toiled in Torah, what other work should they
perform? Let others do the work. This path, however,
did not work for most, who were not as righteous as
Rabbi Shimon. It is impossible for the entire, or even a
majority of the, world to be like Rabbi Shimon.*

*This, then, is why in the second paragraph of the Sh-
ema, when it speaks in the plural form, it does not mention "with all your means." "All your means" implies
a willingness to forfeit all of one's worldly possessions,
and this is not the way for most people, who must have
good financial sense in order to have a livelihood and
be able to live...*

The first paragraph of the Shema is different. It is said in the singular form for singularly saintly individuals; G-d is calling to the likes of Rabbi Shimon to give up everything for Him.

But all of us must still say the first paragraph of the Shema, because a person's initial acceptance of G-dly sovereignty must be accompanied with the approach that he is, indeed, ready to give up all of his possessions, if this is what G-d wants of him...

By the same token, singularly saintly individuals like Rabbi Shimon say the second paragraph as well... Within this world, the Holy One, blessed be He, desired that the world be civilized, and did not create it for chaos. The practice of leaving these boundaries and accepting upon oneself a level of service beyond what the body can handle is behavior from the world of chaos.

4

EKEV

Jewish Apocrypha?

Safeguarding the Purity of Faith

Dedicated in honor of our dear colleague and member of the Torah Studies editorial board,
Rabbi Yaakov Halperin. *May he and his family merit to witness the fulfillment of continuous blessings for health, happiness, nachas and success in all their endeavors.*

PARASHAH OVERVIEW
Ekev

In the Parshah of Eikev ("Because"), Moses continues his closing address to the children of Israel, promising them that if they will fulfill the commandments (mitzvot) of the Torah, they will prosper in the Land *they are about to conquer and settle in keeping with G-d's promise to their forefathers.*

Moses also rebukes *them for their failings in their first generation as a people, recalling their worship of the* Golden Calf, *the rebellion of* Korach, *the sin of the* spies, *their angering of G-d at Taveirah, Massah and Kivrot Hataavah ("*The Graves of Lust*"). "You have been* rebellious *against G-d," he says to them, "since the day I knew you." But he also speaks of G-d's forgiveness of their sins, and the* Second Tablets *which G-d inscribed and gave to them following their repentance.*

Their forty years in the desert, says Moses to the people, during which G-d sustained them with daily manna *from heaven, was to teach them "that man does not live on* bread *alone, but by the* utterance of G-d's mouth *does man live."*

Moses describes the land they are about to enter as "flowing with milk and honey," blessed with the "seven kinds" (wheat, barley, grapevines, figs, pomegranates, olive oil and dates), *and as the place that is the focus of G-d's providence of His world. He commands them to destroy the idols of the land's former masters, and to beware lest they become haughty and begin to believe that "my power and the might of my hand have gotten me this wealth."*

A key passage in our Parshah is the second chapter of the Shema, which repeats the fundamental mitzvot enumerated in the Shema's first chapter, and describes the rewards of fulfilling G-d's commandments and the adverse results (famine and exile) of their neglect. It is also the source of the precept of prayer, and includes a reference to the resurrection of the dead in the messianic age.

Other G-ds

Do Not Stray

TEXT 1

Devarim (Deuteronomy) 11:16

> הִשָּׁמְרוּ לָכֶם פֶּן יִפְתֶּה לְבַבְכֶם וְסַרְתֶּם וַעֲבַדְתֶּם אֱלֹהִים אֲחֵרִים
> וְהִשְׁתַּחֲוִיתֶם לָהֶם:

Take care, in case your heart is seduced away, to turn and worship other gods and bow to them.

TEXT 2

Ibid. 12:30

> הִשָּׁמֶר לְךָ פֶּן תִּנָּקֵשׁ אַחֲרֵיהֶם אַחֲרֵי הִשָּׁמְדָם מִפָּנֶיךָ וּפֶן תִּדְרֹשׁ
> לֵאלֹהֵיהֶם לֵאמֹר אֵיכָה יַעַבְדוּ הַגּוֹיִם הָאֵלֶּה אֶת אֱלֹהֵיהֶם וְאֶעֱשֶׂה כֵּן
> גַּם אָנִי:

Be careful, in case you are lured after their ways after you have destroyed them in front of you, and in case you'll ask after their gods, saying, "How did those nations serve their gods? I will do the same."

A Limit to Learning

TEXT 3

Maimonides, Mishneh Torah, Laws of Idol Worship, 2:2

ספרים רבים חברו עובדי כוכבים בעבודתה היאך עיקר עבודתה
ומה מעשיה ומשפטיה, צוונו הקדוש ברוך הוא שלא לקרות באותן
הספרים כלל ולא נהרהר בה ולא בדבר מדבריה, ואפילו להסתכל
בדמות הצורה אסור שנאמר אל תפנו אל האלילים.
ובענין הזה נאמר ופן תדרוש לאלהיהם לאמר איכה יעבדו שלא
תשאל על דרך עבודתה היאך היא אף על פי שאין אתה עובדה
שדבר זה גורם להפנות אחריה ולעשות כמה שהן עושין שנאמר
ואעשה כן גם אני.

Rabbi Moshe ben Maimon
(Maimonides, Rambam)
1135–1204

Halachist, philosopher, author, and physician. Maimonides was born in Cordoba, Spain. After the conquest of Cordoba by the Almohads, he fled Spain and eventually settled in Cairo, Egypt. There, he became the leader of the Jewish community and served as court physician to the vizier of Egypt. He is most noted for authoring the *Mishneh Torah*, an encyclopedic arrangement of Jewish law, and for his philosophical work, *Guide for the Perplexed*. His rulings on Jewish law are integral to the formation of halachic consensus.

Idol worshippers wrote many books about their worship, how it is performed, its actions, and its laws. The Holy One, Blessed be He, commanded us not to read such books at all, and not to think about them or any of their words. Even to look at the appearance of forms of idols is forbidden, as the verse says, "Do not turn to the idols."

It is about this that the verse also says, "In case you'll ask after their gods, saying, 'How did those nations serve their gods?'" This is forbidden even though you aren't serving idols, since it causes one to turn after them and do as they do, as the verse finishes, "I will do the same."

TEXT 4

Ibid.

ולא עבודת כוכבים בלבד הוא שאסור להפנות אחריה במחשבה אלא כל מחשבה שהוא גורם לו לאדם לעקור עיקר מעיקרי התורה מוזהרין אנו שלא להעלותה על לבנו ולא נסיח דעתנו לכך ונחשוב ונמשך אחר הרהורי הלב, מפני שדעתו של אדם קצרה ולא כל הדעות יכולין להשיג האמת על בוריו, ואם ימשך כל אדם אחר מחשבות לבו נמצא מחריב את העולם לפי קוצר דעתו.

כיצד פעמים יתור אחר עבודת כוכבים ופעמים יחשוב ביחוד הבורא שמא הוא שמא אינו, מה למעלה ומה למטה מה לפנים ומה לאחור, ופעמים בנבואה שמא היא אמת שמא היא אינה, ופעמים בתורה שמא היא מן השמים שמא אינה, ואינו יודע המדות שידין בהן עד שידע האמת על בוריו ונמצא יוצא לידי מינות.

ועל ענין זה הזהירה תורה ונאמר בה "ולא תתורו אחרי לבבכם ואחרי עיניכם אשר אתם זונים", כלומר לא ימשך כל אחד מכם אחר דעתו הקצרה וידמה שמחשבתו משגת האמת, כך אמרו חכמים "אחרי לבבכם זו מינות ואחרי עיניכם זו זנות".

It is not idol worship alone to which one is forbidden to turn, but any thought that causes one to uproot one of the fundamentals of the Torah. We are prohibited from bringing such thoughts to mind, paying attention to them, or allowing our hearts to be drawn after them. Human understanding is limited, and not everyone is able to grasp the truth clearly. If one follows the limited understanding of one's mind, one can come to "destroy the world" through one's ignorance.

In what sense? A person sometimes strays after idol worship, and sometimes thinks about G-d's unity; perhaps He is one, perhaps not. One wonders what is above and what is below, what is before and what is after, and sometimes about prophecy—perhaps it is true and perhaps it isn't—and sometimes about Torah—perhaps it is Divine or perhaps not.

If one doesn't know the right traits that will bring him to the clear truth, they can fall into heresy. This is what the Torah warned about when it said "Do not stray after your hearts and eyes that lead you to immorality." That is to say, you should not be led after your limited understanding and think you have grasped the truth. The Sages say, "After your hearts" refers to heresy, and "after your eyes" refers to immorality.

TEXT 5

Rabbi Yitzchak Abohav, Menorat Ha'Maor, Ner 2, Rule 10, 1:2

Rabbi Yitzchak Abohav
14th century
Preacher and author. Born
in Spain, Rabbi Abohav, a
businessman, was distressed
over the lack of Jewish
scholarship in his time.
Toward the end of his life,
therefore, he dedicated
much time to preaching
and writing. Abohav wrote
Menorat Hama'or, a work
on ethics based on the
aggadic sections of the
Talmud. The work became
a popular household book
in medieval Jewish homes.

וגדולה דבר המינות שאדם צריך לרחקה מלבו, שלא יכנס כלל
אפילו במחשבתו, והזהירה בו תורה יותר מכל העבירות, שנאמר
"ולא תתורו אחרי לבבכם ואחרי עיניכם", ודרשו רז"ל אחרי לבבכם
זו מינות, ואחרי עיניכם זו זנות, כי כל מחשבה רעה שבעולם או
כפירה נכללת במינות, וכל שאר העבירות הבאות מהתאוות נכללות
בזנות, נמצא כי כל האזהרות נכללות במינות וזנות, ובחומרת
המינות הקדימה לזנות.

Heresy is an important matter that a person must distance from his heart, not allowing it even into his thought. The Torah warns us about it more than all other transgressions, as the verse states, "Do not stray after your hearts and eyes." The Sages explained it: "After your hearts," this is heresy; "And after your eyes," this is immorality.

Every evil system of thought or apostasy is included in heresy, and all of the transgressions deriving from lusts are included in immorality. Therefore, all of the Torah's bans are included in heresy and immorality. But so serious is heresy that in the verse it precedes immorality!

When May One Philosophize?

TEXT 6A

Rabbi Yitzchak bar Sheshet, Responsa of the Rivash, Section 45

אמנם, ספרי הטבע המפורסמים, לא מן השם הוא זה, אבל ראוי
לימנע מהם, אם הם מתאמצים לעקור עקרי תורתינו הקדושה.
ובפרט שני עמודי התוך אשר היא נכונה עליהם, שזהו, חדוש
העולם, והשגחת השם יתברך בפרטי המין האנושי. והם מביאים
ראיות ומופתים לפי דעתם לקיים קדמות העולם, ושהוא מחוייב
מן השם יתברך, כמו שהאור מחוייב מן השמש, והצל מן האילן, ואין
יכולת לשם יתברך לשנות דבר מטבעו, ולא להאריך כנף הזבוב, ולא
לקצר רגל הנמלה; כמו שאין יכולת בשמש לשנות האור הנמשך
ממנו, ולא האילן הצל. וכן, שהשגחת השם יתברך לא תהיה במה
שהוא למטה מגלגל הירח.

וכתבו בספריהם, שאין ידיעה שלמה רק אותה שהיא מצד החקירה,
לא מצד הקבלה. ואנחנו מקבלי האמת, דעתנו, שהתורה שלנו
שלמה, שבאה אלינו במעמד הר סיני מפי הגבורה ובאמצעות אדון
הנביאים ע"ה, היא למעלה מהכל, וכל חקירתם אפס ותהו לערכה.

Rabbi Yitzchak Perfet
(Rivash, Rabbi Yitzchak
ben Sheshet)
1326–1408
Halachist. Rivash studied
under Rabbeinu Nisim of
Gerona (Ran) in Barcelona,
and served as rabbi there
and in other important
Jewish communities in Spain.
Because of the eruption of
anti-Jewish riots in 1391,
he fled to North Africa
and settled in Algiers. He
was the first to address the
halachic status of Marranos.
Rivash's Halachic responsa
are his most important
work; the contain sources
no longer extant and served,
in part, as a basis for the
Code of Jewish Law.

The famous works of natural philosophy are not G-dly, and it is appropriate to avoid them if they endeavor to uproot the main truths of our holy Torah.

Specifically, they undermine the two fundamental pillars of Judaism: that is, that the world was created, and that G-d exerts providence over the lives of individual human beings. The philosophers cite proofs and examples that in their opinion demonstrate that the world has existed forever, and that G-d must necessarily create the world as it is, just as light naturally flows from the sun and a tree naturally casts a shadow. They argue that G-d cannot alter nature in any way, cannot lengthen the wing of the fly or shorten the leg of the ant, just as the sun cannot change its own light or the tree its own shadow. They argue further that G-d's providence does not extend to below the sphere of the moon.

They write in their works that no knowledge is perfect except that of philosophy, not even revelation. However, we Jews are the receivers of the revealed truth, and our position is that our Torah is perfect and was revealed to the assembly at Mount Sinai from the mouth of G-d Himself and through the master of the prophets. The Torah stands above all, and all philosophies are emptiness and chaos in comparison.

TEXT 6B

Ibid.

ואין להביא ראיה מהרמב״ם ז״ל. כי הוא למד קודם לכן כל התורה כולה בשלמות, הלכות ואגדות, תוספתא, ספרא וספרי וכוליה תלמודא, בבלי וירושלמי, כמו שנראה מספר משנה תורה שחבר. וכדי להשיב את האפיקורוס, עשה ספר המורה, לסתור המופתים והראיות שהביא הפילוסוף לקיים קדמות העולם, וכן בעניין ההשגחה. ולפי שהיו בזמנו הרבה מישראל נבוכים בעקרי התורה, מפני מה שלמדו מן החכמה ההיא.

One should not look to the Rambam, of blessed memory, as an example. The Rambam was exceptional; before he set out to study philosophy, he first studies the rest of Torah completely, its laws and stories, the Tosefta, Sifra, and Sifri, etc., as well as the entire Talmuds, both the Babylonian and Jerusalem Talmud, as we see from his book the Mishneh Torah.

It was only in order to counter the heretics that he then wrote The Guide, to counter their examples and proofs used to prove the eternity of the world and the lack of G-d's providence. He did this because in his time, many Jews were confused about the most important truths of the Torah, precisely because they had learned modern philosophy.

The Outside Texts

What Are the Apocrypha?

Tosefta
A compendium of laws similar in format to that of the Mishnah; it consists of teachings of the sages of the Mishnah. At times, the material in both works is similar; at other times, there are significant differences between the two. The Talmud often compares these texts in its analysis. According to tradition, the *Tosefta* was redacted by Rabbis Chiyah and Oshiyah in the beginning of the 3rd century in the Land of Israel.

TEXT 7

Tosefta, Tractate Sotah, 13:3

> משמתו נביאים האחרונים חגי זכריה ומלאכי פסקה רוח הקודש מישראל.

From the time of the deaths of the final prophets, Haggai, Zechariah, and Malachi, the holy spirit of Divine Inspiration left the Children of Israel.

A Nuanced Approach

TEXT 8

Talmud Tractate Sanhedrin, 100b

Babylonian Talmud
A literary work of monumental proportions that draws upon the legal, spiritual, intellectual, ethical, and historical traditions of Judaism. The 37 tractates of the Babylonian Talmud contain the teachings of the Jewish sages from the period after the destruction of the 2nd Temple through the 5th century CE. It has served as the primary vehicle for the transmission of the Oral Law and the education of Jews over the centuries; it is the entry point for all subsequent legal, ethical, and theological Jewish scholarship.

> רבי עקיבא אומר: אף הקורא בספרים החיצונים וכו'. תנא: בספרי מינים. רב יוסף אמר: בספר בן סירא נמי אסור למיקרי.

Rabbi Akiva says: One who reads the external literature also has no share in the World to Come. The Sages taught in a Beraita: This refers to reading the works of heretics. Rav Yosef says: It is also prohibited to read the book of Ben Sira.

TEXT 9

Talmud Tractate Baba Kama, 92b

מטייל ואזיל דיקלא בישא גבי קינא דשרכי? אמר ליה: דבר זה
כתוב בתורה, שנוי בנביאים, ומשולש בכתובים...
כתוב בתורה, דכתיב: וילך עשו אל ישמעאל, שנוי בנביאים דכתיב:
ויתלקטו אל יפתח אנשים רקים ויהיו עמו; ומשולש בכתובים,
דכתיב: כל עוף למינו ישכון ובני אדם לדומה לו.

From where is the matter derived that people say, "A bad palm tree goes to be among a grove of barren trees," that is, that bad people seek out bad neighbors? He responded: This matter is written in the Torah, repeated in the Prophets, and repeated a third time in the Writings…

In Torah, as it is written, "And Esau went to Yishmael." Repeated in Prophets, as it is written, "And the vain people were gathered to Yiftach and went with him." Repeated a third time, as it is written, "All fowl lives with its kind, and all men with those like him."

TEXT 10

Rabbi Yomtov Asevilli, Chiddushei Haritva, Tractate Baba Batra 98b

Rabbi Yomtov Asevilli
(Ritva)
ca. 1250–1330
Spanish rabbi and Talmudist.
Ritva was born in Seville.
He is mostly known for
his Talmudic commentary,
which is extremely clear, and
to this day, remains most
frequently quoted and used.

אַף עַל פִּי שקראוהו בסנהדרין ספרים החצונים, שמע מינה שלא אסרו שם אלא לעשות ממנו קבע אבל ראוי להגות בו בעתות ללמוד ממנו חכמה ומוסר, מה שאין כן בספרי מינין ממש.

Tractate Sanhedrin seems to imply that the External Literature is tantamount to heresy?! One must conclude that the intent there is to outlaw one to canonize the External Literature as part of Tanach, or as Holy Works. It is, however, appropriate at times to study them in order to learn wisdom or ethical direction, unlike literal works of heresy.

Tale of Two Presses

TEXT 11

Rabbi Shneur Zalman of Liadi, Igrot Kodesh #55

ולזאת אמינא לפעולא טבא יישר חילא לאורייתא והנני פותח פתח
לרווחה לכבוד הרב הנ"ל בגדר שגדרו גאוני דורינו בהסכמותיהם
על הדפסת ש"ס וד' טורים חנ"ל שנדפסו מקרוב בק' הנ"ל, שגדרו
וגזרו בגזרת עירין על שאר כל המדפיסים ועל כללות עם בני
ישראל, שלא לחזור ולהדפיס הש"ס או הד' טורים עד תום משך
כ"ח שנים מחתחלת הדפוס הנ"ל ומעתח [הנה] כל יפוי [כח וזכות]
מהסכמות הגאונים הנ"ל נתונים נתונים המה לכבוד הרב הנ"ל וב"כ,
שחלילה חלילה לשום בר ישראל להשיג גבולו ח"ו, לחזור ולהדפיס
הש"ס או הד' טורים בשום תחבולה וערמה בעולם עד כלות הזמן
אשר נבלו הגאונים הנ"ל בהסכמותיהם חנ"ל. וכל המשיג גבולו ח"ו
יהיה נידון בכלל ארור משיג גבול רעהו, וארור בו קללה בו וכו' ח"ו,
כנודע ממאמרז"ל.

**Rabbi Shneur
Zalman of Liadi
(Alter Rebbe)**
1745–1812

Chasidic rebbe, halachic
authority, and founder of
the Chabad movement. The
Alter Rebbe was born in
Liozna, Belarus, and was
among the principal students
of the Magid of Mezeritch.
His numerous works include
the *Tanya*, an early classic
containing the fundamentals
of Chabad Chasidism, and
Shulchan Aruch HaRav,
an expanded and reworked
code of Jewish law.

And therefore, for his good work, may his strength in Torah increase! I hereby throw open the doors for their livelihood with regard to the boundary established by the Torah masters of our generation with their approbations on his printing of the Talmud and the Tur that he is currently publishing. Their boundary and their decree fell on all printing houses and the entire Jewish people, not to reprint this Talmud or Tur for twenty-five years, from the time it was first printed, as mentioned above. And now, all the beauty, power, and merit of their approbations are all given over to the respectable Rabbi Moshe, that G-d forbid any Jew should touch what is not his and reprint the Talmud or Tur, regardless of scheme or deception, until the end of the time those Torah masters established in their approbations. And anyone who trespasses on Rabbi Moshe's domain will be considered to be in violation of the verse, "Cursed is the one who moves his neighbor's border." Such a person truly is cursed and unfortunate, G-d-forbid, as is known from the words of the Sages.

TEXT 12

Words of Rabbi Yissachar Dov Rokeach of Belz,
"Kadosh U'Baruch" p. 42

ספרי סלאוויאט חלה עליהם קדושה כעין קדושת ספר תורה.

The holy books published in Slavita have a sanctity similar to that of a Torah scroll.

TEXT 13

Letter of Rabbi Akiva Eiger

מאוד הומה לבי על העזות והחוצפה של מדפיסי סלאוויטא,
ודבריהם דברי נאצה הם, לא בלבד על בני הגאון נר"ו שהטה את
לבבי, אלא גם עלי, שיכולים לפתות אותי לפסוק שלא כדין.....
איני מוחל להם כלל וכלל, כי על בזיון התורה אי אפשר למחול.

Rabbi Akiva Eiger
1761–1837
Born in Eisenstaedt, Hungary;
an outstanding talmudic
scholar and influential
halachic decisor. Authored
commentaries on the
Talmud and the Shulchan
Aruch. Was rabbi of the
city of Posen. His daughter
married the Chatam Sofer.

I am shocked by the insolence and brazenness of the Slavita printers and their hateful words, not only that my son persuaded me, but also that I myself have been taken in and persuaded to rule incorrectly...I do not forgive them for this at all, because one cannot forgive an affront to the Torah itself.

5

Re'eh

Pick a Side

The Peril of Indecision

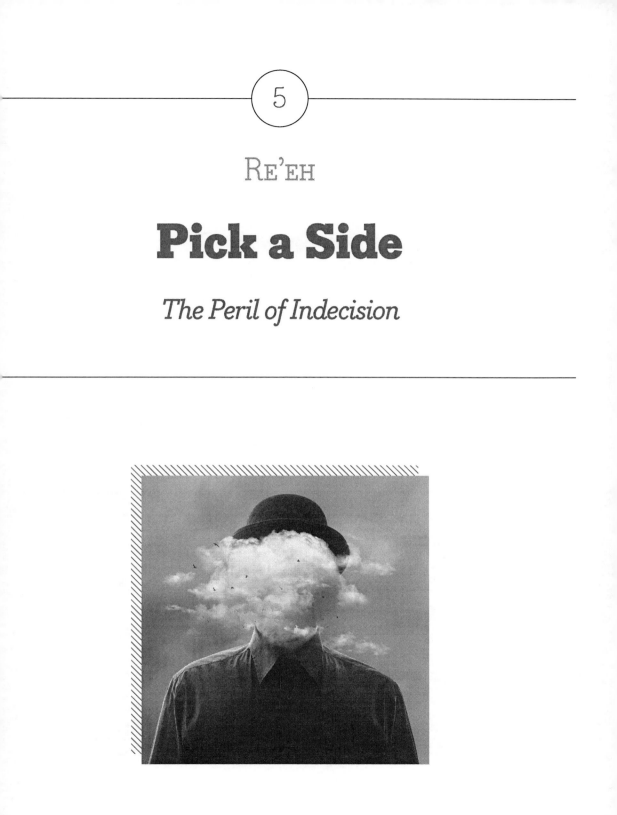

Dedicated in honor of our dear colleague and member of the Torah Studies editorial board,
Rabbi Nechemia Schusterman. May he and his family merit to witness the fulfillment of continuous
blessings for health, happiness, nachas and success in all their endeavors.

PARASHAH OVERVIEW
Re'eh

"See," says Moses to the people of Israel, "I place before you today a blessing and a curse"—the blessing that will come when they fulfill G-d's commandments, and the curse if they abandon them. These should be proclaimed on Mount Gerizim and Mount Ebal when the people cross over into the Holy Land.

A Temple should be established in "the place that G-d will choose to make dwell His name there," where the people should bring their sacrifices to Him; it is forbidden to make offerings to G-d in any other place. It is permitted to slaughter animals elsewhere, not as a sacrifice but to eat their meat; the blood (which in the Temple is poured upon the altar), however, may not be eaten.

A false prophet, or one who entices others to worship idols, should be put to death; an idolatrous city must be destroyed. The identifying signs for kosher animals and fish, and the list of non-kosher birds (first given in Leviticus 11), are repeated.

A tenth of all produce is to be eaten in Jerusalem, or else exchanged for money with which food is purchased and eaten there. In certain years this tithe is given to the poor instead. Firstborn cattle and sheep are to be offered in the Temple, and their meat eaten by the kohanim (priests).

The mitzvah of charity obligates a Jew to aid a needy fellow with a gift or loan. On the Sabbatical year (occurring every seventh year), all loans are to be forgiven. All indentured servants are to be set free after six years of service.

Our Parshah concludes with the laws of the three pilgrimage festivals—Passover, Shavuot and Sukkot—when all should go to "see and be seen" before G-d in the Holy Temple.

Eliyahu's Contest

Sacrifice Central

TEXT 1

Devarim (Deuteronomy) 12:11-14

וְהָיָה הַמָּקוֹם אֲשֶׁר יִבְחַר ה' אֱלֹקֵיכֶם בּוֹ לְשַׁכֵּן שְׁמוֹ שָׁם שָׁמָּה תָבִיאוּ
אֵת כָּל אֲשֶׁר אָנֹכִי מְצַוֶּה אֶתְכֶם עוֹלֹתֵיכֶם וְזִבְחֵיכֶם מַעְשְׂרֹתֵיכֶם
וּתְרֻמַת יֶדְכֶם וְכֹל מִבְחַר נִדְרֵיכֶם אֲשֶׁר תִּדְּרוּ לַה':
וּשְׂמַחְתֶּם לִפְנֵי ה' אֱלֹקֵיכֶם אַתֶּם וּבְנֵיכֶם וּבְנֹתֵיכֶם וְעַבְדֵיכֶם
וְאַמְהֹתֵיכֶם וְהַלֵּוִי אֲשֶׁר בְּשַׁעֲרֵיכֶם כִּי אֵין לוֹ חֵלֶק וְנַחֲלָה אִתְּכֶם:
הִשָּׁמֶר לְךָ פֶּן תַּעֲלֶה עֹלֹתֶיךָ בְּכָל מָקוֹם אֲשֶׁר תִּרְאֶה:
כִּי אִם בַּמָּקוֹם אֲשֶׁר יִבְחַר ה' בְּאַחַד שְׁבָטֶיךָ שָׁם תַּעֲלֶה עֹלֹתֶיךָ וְשָׁם
תַּעֲשֶׂה כֹּל אֲשֶׁר אָנֹכִי מְצַוֶּךָּ:

And it will be, that the place the Lord, your G-d, will choose in which to establish His Name there you shall bring all that I am commanding you: Your burnt offerings, and your sacrifices, your tithes, and the separation by your hand, and the choice of vows that you will vow to G-d.

And you shall rejoice before the Lord, your G-d, you and your sons and your daughters and your menservants and your maidservants, and the Levite who is within your cities, for he has no portion or inheritance with you.

Beware, lest you offer up your burnt offerings any place you see.

But only in the place G-d will choose in one of your tribes—there you shall offer up your burnt offerings, and there you shall do all that I command you.

TEXT 2

Maimonides, Mishneh Torah, Ma'aseh Hakorbanot 18:1

המקריב קרבן חוץ לעזרה ביטל מצות עשה ועבר על לא תעשה שנאמר השמר לך פן תעלה עולותיך בכל מקום אשר תראה, ואם הקריב במזיד חייב כרת שנאמר אשר יעלה עולה או זבח ואל פתח אהל מועד לא הביאו ונכרת מעמיו, בשוגג מביא חטאת קבועה.

One who offers a sacrifice outside the Temple courtyard negates a positive commandment and violates a negative commandment, as the verse states, "Take heed lest you offer your burnt-offerings in any place that you see." If he offered a sacrifice in such a place willfully, he is liable for karet, *as the verse states, "[Any man]... who will offer a burnt-offering or a sacrifice, but did not bring it to the Tent of Meeting... he will be cut off from his people." If he transgressed unknowingly, he must bring a fixed sin-offering.*

Rabbi Moshe ben Maimon
(Maimonides, Rambam)
1135–1204

Halachist, philosopher, author, and physician. Maimonides was born in Cordoba, Spain. After the conquest of Cordoba by the Almohads, he fled Spain and eventually settled in Cairo, Egypt. There, he became the leader of the Jewish community and served as court physician to the vizier of Egypt. He is most noted for authoring the *Mishneh Torah*, an encyclopedic arrangement of Jewish law, and for his philosophical work, *Guide for the Perplexed*. His rulings on Jewish law are integral to the formation of halachic consensus.

The Importance of a Designated Place

TEXT 3

Rabbi Aharon Halevi of Barcelona,
Sefer Hachinuch, Mitzvah 440

**Rabbi Aharon Halevi
of Barcelona**
(Re'ah)
1235–1290

Born in Gerona, Spain. Rabbi,
talmudist, and authority on
Jewish law. Rabbi Aharon
studied under Nachmanides
and under his father,
Rabbi Yosef Halevi, and
corresponded with the leading
talmudic scholars of his
generation. His explanations
on the Rashba's halachic
code, *Torat Habayit*, entitled
Bedek Habayit, are integral
in the formation of Jewish
law. Rabbi Aharon was
considered by some to be the
anonymous author of *Sefer
Hachinuch*, a compendium
of the 613 commandments.

משרשי המצוה, כי בהיות מקום מיוחד בעולם לקרבנות וההתמדה
בו לבקש משם את ה' אלקיך יתקדש המקום ונחה עליו רצון האל
ושפע ברכתו שופע עליו תמיד, ויהיו לבבות בני אדם מתפחדים
ומתרככים לזכרו וישוב כל איש מדרכו הרעה ומן החמס אשר
בכפיו בראותו אותו, ואם כל המקומות יוכשרו להקרבה לא יהיה
כן בכולן ידוע הדבר.

*The reason for this mitzvah: When there is one des-
ignated place for sacrifices, where the Jewish people
always go to seek G-d, that place will be sanctified, and
G-d's will and blessing will be bestowed upon it always.
The heart will be awed and softened in that place, so
that every person will return from his evil ways and
from his unjust deeds. If it was permissible to bring
sacrifices in any place, this would not be the case.*

Eliyahu's Showdown

TEXT 4A

Melachim I (1 Kings) 18:19-24

וְעַתָּה שְׁלַח קְבֹץ אֵלַי אֶת כָּל יִשְׂרָאֵל אֶל הַר הַכַּרְמֶל וְאֶת נְבִיאֵי
הַבַּעַל אַרְבַּע מֵאוֹת וַחֲמִשִּׁים וּנְבִיאֵי הָאֲשֵׁרָה אַרְבַּע מֵאוֹת אֹכְלֵי
שֻׁלְחַן אִיזָבֶל:
וַיִּשְׁלַח אַחְאָב בְּכָל בְּנֵי יִשְׂרָאֵל וַיִּקְבֹּץ אֶת הַנְּבִיאִים אֶל הַר הַכַּרְמֶל:
וַיִּגַּשׁ אֵלִיָּהוּ אֶל כָּל הָעָם וַיֹּאמֶר עַד מָתַי אַתֶּם פֹּסְחִים עַל שְׁתֵּי
הַסְּעִפִּים אִם ה' הָאֱלֹקִים לְכוּ אַחֲרָיו וְאִם הַבַּעַל לְכוּ אַחֲרָיו וְלֹא עָנוּ
הָעָם אֹתוֹ דָּבָר:
וַיֹּאמֶר אֵלִיָּהוּ אֶל הָעָם אֲנִי נוֹתַרְתִּי נָבִיא לַה' לְבַדִּי וּנְבִיאֵי הַבַּעַל
אַרְבַּע מֵאוֹת וַחֲמִשִּׁים אִישׁ:
וְיִתְּנוּ לָנוּ שְׁנַיִם פָּרִים וְיִבְחֲרוּ לָהֶם הַפָּר הָאֶחָד וִינַתְּחֻהוּ וְיָשִׂימוּ עַל
הָעֵצִים וְאֵשׁ לֹא יָשִׂימוּ וַאֲנִי אֶעֱשֶׂה אֶת הַפָּר הָאֶחָד וְנָתַתִּי עַל הָעֵצִים
וְאֵשׁ לֹא אָשִׂים:
וּקְרָאתֶם בְּשֵׁם אֱלֹהֵיכֶם וַאֲנִי אֶקְרָא בְשֵׁם ה' וְהָיָה הָאֱלֹהִים אֲשֶׁר
יַעֲנֶה בָאֵשׁ הוּא הָאֱלֹהִים וַיַּעַן כָּל הָעָם וַיֹּאמְרוּ טוֹב הַדָּבָר:

And now, send and gather for me all of Israel to Mount Carmel, and the prophets of the Baal four hundred and fifty, and the prophets of the Ashera four hundred who eat at Jezebel's table.

And Ahab sent among all of the Children of Israel, and he gathered the prophets to Mount Carmel.

And Elijah drew near to all the people and said, "Until when are you hopping between two ideas? If the Lord is G-d, go after Him, and if the Baal, go after him." And the people did not answer him a word.

And Elijah spoke to the people, "I have remained a prophet to G-d by myself, and the prophets of the Baal are four hundred and fifty men.

"And let them give us two bulls and let them choose one bull for themselves and cut it up and place it on the wood, but fire they shall not put, and I will prepare one bull, and I will put it on the wood, and fire will I not place.

"And you will call in the name of your deity, and I will call in the name of G-d, and it will be the God that will answer with fire, he is God." And all of the people answered and said, "The thing is good."

TEXT 4B

Ibid. 36-39

וַיְהִי בַּעֲלוֹת הַמִּנְחָה וַיִּגַּשׁ אֵלִיָּהוּ הַנָּבִיא וַיֹּאמַר ה' אֱלֹקֵי אַבְרָהָם יִצְחָק
וְיִשְׂרָאֵל הַיּוֹם יִוָּדַע כִּי אַתָּה אֱלֹקִים בְּיִשְׂרָאֵל וַאֲנִי עַבְדֶּךָ וּבִדְבָרְךָ
עָשִׂיתִי אֵת כָּל הַדְּבָרִים הָאֵלֶּה:
עֲנֵנִי ה' עֲנֵנִי וְיֵדְעוּ הָעָם הַזֶּה כִּי אַתָּה ה' הָאֱלֹקִים וְאַתָּה הֲסִבֹּתָ אֶת
לִבָּם אֲחֹרַנִּית:
וַתִּפֹּל אֵשׁ ה' וַתֹּאכַל אֶת הָעֹלָה וְאֶת הָעֵצִים וְאֶת הָאֲבָנִים וְאֶת הֶעָפָר
וְאֶת הַמַּיִם אֲשֶׁר בַּתְּעָלָה לִחֵכָה:
וַיַּרְא כָּל הָעָם וַיִּפְּלוּ עַל פְּנֵיהֶם וַיֹּאמְרוּ ה' הוּא הָאֱלֹקִים ה'
הוּא הָאֱלֹקִים:

And it was when the evening sacrifice was offered that Elijah the prophet came near and said, "Lord, the G-d of Abraham, Isaac, and Israel, today let it be known that You are G-d in Israel and that I am Your servant, and at Your word have I done all these things.

"Answer me, O G-d, answer me, and this people shall know that You are the Lord G-d, and You have turned their hearts backward."

And the fire of G-d fell and consumed the burnt offerings and the wood and the stones and the earth, and the water that was in the trench it licked up.

And all the people saw and fell on their faces, and they said, "The Lord is G-d, the Lord is G-d."

How Could He?

TEXT 5A

Maimonides, Mishneh Torah, Hilchot Yesodei Hatorah 9:1

דבר ברור ומפורש בתורה שהיא מצוה עומדת לעולם ולעולמי
עולמים אין לה לא שינוי ולא גרעון ולא תוספת שנאמר את כל
הדבר אשר אנכי מצוה אתכם אותו תשמרון לעשות לא תוסף עליו
ולא תגרע ממנו...

וכן הוא אומר חוקת עולם לדורותיכם, ונאמר לא בשמים היא, הא
למדת שאין נביא רשאי לחדש דבר מעתה, לפיכך אם יעמוד איש
בין מן האומות בין מישראל ויעשה אות ומופת ויאמר שה' שלחו
להוסיף מצוה או לגרוע מצוה או לפרש במצוה מן המצות פירוש
שלא שמענו ממשה, או שאמר שאותן המצות שנצטוו בהן ישראל
אינן לעולם ולדורי דורות אלא מצות לפי זמן היו, הרי זה נביא שקר
שהרי בא להכחיש נבואתו של משה, ומיתתו בחנק על שהזיד
לדבר בשם ה' אשר לא צוהו.

*It is clear and explicit in the Torah that G-d's command
remain forever without change, amendment, or dimin-
ishment, as the verse states, "All these matters that I
command to you, you shall be careful to perform. You
may not add to it or diminish from it…" It is also said,
"It is an everlasting statute for all your generations,"
and the verse states further, "It is not in the heavens."
This teaches that a prophet can no longer add a new
precept [to the Torah].*

Therefore, if a person will arise, whether Jew or gentile, and perform a sign or wonder and say that G-d sent him to: add a mitzvah, withdraw a mitzvah explain a mitzvah in a manner that differs from the tradition received from Moses, or if he says that the mitzvot commanded to the Jews are not forever, but rather were given for a limited time, he is a false prophet. He comes to deny the prophecy of Moses and should be executed by strangulation, because he dared to make statements in G-d's name that G-d never made.

Emergency Circumstances

TEXT 5B

Ibid. 9:3

> וכן אם יאמר לנו הנביא שנודע לנו שהוא נביא לעבור על אחת מכל
> מצות האמורות בתורה או על מצות הרבה בין קלות בין חמורות
> לפי שעה מצוה לשמוע לו.

When a proven prophet instructs us to violate a single mitzvah of the Torah or many mitzvot, whether they are of a severe or light nature, for a limited amount of time, it is a mitzvah to listen to him.

TEXT 5C

Ibid.

וכן למדנו מחכמים ראשונים מפי השמועה בכל אם יאמר לך
הנביא עבור על דברי תורה כאליהו בהר הכרמל שמע לו חוץ
מעבודת כוכבים, והוא שיהיה הדבר לפי שעה, כגון אליהו בהר
הכרמל שהקריב בחוץ וירושלים נבחרת לכך והמקריב
בחוץ חייב כרת, ומפני שהוא נביא מצוה לשמוע לו וגם בזה נאמר
אליו תשמעון, ואילו שאלו את אליהו ואמרו לו היאך נעקור מ"ש
בתורה...היה אומר לא נאמר אלא המקריב בחוץ לעולם חייב כרת
כמו שצוה משה, אבל אני אקריב היום בחוץ בדבר ה' כדי להכחיש
נביאי הבעל, ועל הדרך הזאת אם צוו כל הנביאים לעבור לפי שעה
מצוה לשמוע להם, ואם אמרו שהדבר נעקר לעולם מיתתו בחנק
שהתורה אמרה לנו ולבנינו עד עולם.

The Sages of the early generation taught as part of the Oral Tradition: If a prophet tells you to violate the precepts of the Torah as Elijah did on Mount Carmel, listen to him with regard to all things except the worship of false gods. This only applies when his command is temporary in nature. For example, on Mount Carmel, Elijah offered a sacrifice outside the Temple, even though Jerusalem was chosen for such service, and one who offers a sacrifice outside the Temple is liable for karet. *Since he was [already established as] a prophet, it was a mitzvah to listen to him. The commandment "Listen to him" applies in these circumstances as well. If they would have asked Elijah: How can we violate the Torah's command... he would have told them,*

"One who offers a sacrifice outside the Temple as if it were always permissible is liable for karet, as Moses said. But I am only offering a sacrifice today outside the Temple at G-d's command in order to disprove the prophets of Baal." Similarly, if any other prophet commands us to transgress for a limited time, it is a mitzvah to listen to him. If, however, he says that the mitzvah has been nullified forever, he is liable for execution by strangulation, for the Torah has told us, "[It is] for us and our children forever."

The Blame Game

Straddling the Fence

TEXT 6

Melachim I (I Kings) 18:21

וַיִּגַּשׁ אֵלִיָּהוּ אֶל כָּל הָעָם וַיֹּאמֶר עַד מָתַי אַתֶּם פֹּסְחִים עַל שְׁתֵּי הַסְּעִפִּים אִם ה׳ הָאֱלֹקִים לְכוּ אַחֲרָיו וְאִם הַבַּעַל לְכוּ אַחֲרָיו וְלֹא עָנוּ הָעָם אֹתוֹ דָּבָר:

And Elijah drew near to all the people and said, "How long will you hop between the two ideas? If the Lord is G-d, go after Him, and if the Baal, go after him." And the people did not answer him a word.

TEXT 7

The Lubavitcher Rebbe, Likutei Sichot vol 1, p.183

לכאורה, פארוואס האט ער ביי זיי געמאַנט עד מתי אתם פוסחים
על שתי הסעיפים, ער האט געדאַרפט מאָנען עד מתי אתם עובדים
לבעל, שוין צייט איר זאלט אויפהערן דינען דעם בעל און אנהויבן
זאָגן הוי' הוא האלקים!

Why did he challenge them, "Until when are you hopping between two ideas?" Shouldn't he have said, "How long will you worship the Baal? The time has come to stop and say, 'The Lord is G-d!'"

Rabbi Menachem Mendel Schneerson
1902–1994

The towering Jewish leader of the 20th century, known as "the Lubavitcher Rebbe," or simply as "the Rebbe." Born in southern Ukraine, the Rebbe escaped Nazi-occupied Europe, arriving in the U.S. in June 1941. The Rebbe inspired and guided the revival of traditional Judaism after the European devastation, impacting virtually every Jewish community the world over. The Rebbe often emphasized that the performance of just one additional good deed could usher in the era of Mashiach. The Rebbe's scholarly talks and writings have been printed in more than 200 volumes.

The Provisional Guilt Offering

TEXT 8

Rabbi Yonah of Gerona, commentary to Ri"f, Berachot 1b

Rabbi Yonah of Gerona
d. 1263

Spanish rabbi and Talmudist. Rabbeinu Yonah from Gerona, Catalonia, was a cousin of Nachmanides. He is renowned for his outspoken critique of Maimonides' works, and for later recanting his opposition and vowing to travel to Maimonides' grave in Israel to beg his forgiveness. He left France, but was detained in Toledo, Spain, where he stayed and became one of the greatest Talmudists of his time. He is best known for his moralistic works on repentance and asceticism.

שעונש הספק יותר מהודאי... ואם מביא אשם על הספק כגון שהיו
לפניו ב' חתיכות אחת של שומן ואחת של חלב ואכל אחת מהן
ואינו יודע איזה מהן אכל צריך להביא ב' סלעים שהם מ"ח מעין...
ועל הודאי סגי במעה א' בלבד.

והטעם בזה למה החמירו על הספק יותר מן הודאי אומר מורי
הרב שהוא מפני שעל הודאי משים האדם החטא אל לבו ודואג
ומתחרט עליו וחוזר בתשובה שלימה אבל על הספק עושה סברות
ואומר אותה חתיכה שאכלתי אולי היתה מותרת ולא ישית אל לבו
לשוב ולזה החמירו בו יותר.

The punishment for a case of possible sin is greater than the punishment for a definite sin… as in the case of the one who brings a provisional guilt-offering. For example: If there were two pieces of fatty meat in front of him, of which one was shuman-*fat [which is permissible] and the other* cheilev-*fat [which is prohibited], and he doesn't know which piece he ate, his offering must then be worth at least two* selas, *which are equal to forty-eight* ma'ahs. *For a definite sin, by contrast, an offering worth one* ma'ah *suffices.*

My master and teacher explained why a case of doubt is more severe than a case of definite sin: When one knows he has committed a sin, he takes it to heart and the matter concerns him. He therefore regrets his deed and repents completely. But if one is unsure if he has in fact committed a sin, he considers that perhaps indeed he only ate the permissible piece of meat. Consequently, the matter doesn't concern him enough to repent. Therefore, the punishment for such a case is greater.

Avoiding Blame

TEXT 9A

Rabbi Shalom Dovber of Lubavitch,
Kuntres Uma'ayan Discourse 14, ch. 2

וּפְעוּלַת הַהַצְדָּקָה הַלָּזוּ שֶׁמַּצְדִּיק אֶת עַצְמוֹ הוּא שֶׁאֵין תְּשׁוּבָתוֹ כִּדְבָעֵי לְמֶהֱוֵי... שֶׁאֵין הַחֲרָטָה עַל הֶעָבָר וְהַקַּבָּלָה עַל לְהַבָּא אֲמִיתִּית כָּל כָּךְ, כִּי הַחֲרָטָה וְהַקַּבָּלָה תְּלוּיוֹת בִּמְרִירוּת נַפְשׁוֹ, דְּכַאֲשֶׁר מִתְמַרְמֵר בְּנַפְשׁוֹ מְאֹד עַל הַחֵטְא וְהֶעָוֹן, אָז הוּא מִתְחָרֵט בֶּאֱמֶת וְעוֹקֵר רְצוֹנוֹ לְגַמְרֵי מִזֶּה וּמִמֵּילָא הַקַּבָּלָה עַל לְהַבָּא אֲמִיתִּית, אֲבָל עַל יְדֵי שֶׁמַּצְדִּיק אֶת עַצְמוֹ הֲרֵי אֵין מְרִירוּת נַפְשׁוֹ גְּדוֹלָה כָּל כָּךְ, מֵאַחַר שֶׁמּוֹצֵא זְכוּת עַל עַצְמוֹ, וּמֵאַחַר שֶׁהַמְּרִירוּת אֵינָהּ גְּדוֹלָה כָּל כָּךְ מִמֵּילָא הַחֲרָטָה וְהַקַּבָּלָה אֵינָם אֲמִיתִּים.

Rabbi Shalom Dovber Schneersohn (Rashab)
1860–1920

Chasidic rebbe. Rabbi Shalom Dovber became the fifth leader of the Chabad movement upon the passing of his father, Rabbi Shmuel of Lubavitch. He established the Lubavitch network of *yeshivot* called Tomchei Temimim. He authored many volumes of chasidic discourses and is renowned for his lucid and thorough explanations of kabbalistic concepts.

The result of self-justification is that one's repentance is incomplete… Any regret for his deed and positive resolution for the future will not be so genuine, for regret and positive resolutions depend on how bitter one feels about his sin. When one really feels bitter about his sin, he will truly regret it, and completely uproot any desire for that sin. Automatically, his positive resolution will be sincere. But by self-justification, he doesn't feel such bitterness, for he finds excuses for himself. Once that bitterness is not there, any regret and positive resolution will not be sincere.

TEXT 9B

Ibid.

וּבִפְרָט אֶחָד הֲרֵי זֶה יוֹתֵר גָּרוּעַ מִשְּׁטוּת הַקּוֹדֶם, כִּי הֲרֵי לְאַחַר שֶׁכְּבָר עָבַר עֲבֵירָה רַחֲמָנָא לִצְלָן כְּשֶׁעוֹשֶׂה תְּשׁוּבָה מֵעוּמְקָא דְלִיבָּא הֲרֵי אָמְרוּ מָקוֹם שֶׁבַּעֲלֵי תְּשׁוּבָה עוֹמְדִים צַדִּיקִים גְּמוּרִים אֵינָן עוֹמְדִין, וַהֲרֵי הַשְּׁטוּת הַזֶּה מוֹנֵעַ אוֹתוֹ מִזֶּה, אִם כֵּן הֲרֵי שְׁטוּת זֶה עוֹד גָּרוּעַ יוֹתֵר שֶׁחוֹשֵׁךְ וּמוֹנֵעַ אוֹתוֹ מִטּוֹבָה הַרְבֵּה, שֶׁעַל יְדֵי תְּשׁוּבָתוֹ הָאֲמִיתִּית הָיָה בָּא לְמַעֲלָה וּמַדְרֵיגָה גְּבוֹהַּ מְאֹד.

In one respect, this [self-justification] is worse than the foolishness that brought one to sin in the first place. For once one has already committed a sin, G-d forbid, through repentance he can reach new heights, as the Sages taught, "In the place where baalei teshuvah stand, even the completely righteous are unable to stand." But self-justification precludes this, and is therefore even worse for it prevents one from much good—for through sincere teshuvah he could have attained a very high spiritual level.

Idolatry and Straddling the Fence Today

Ideology of Idolatry

TEXT 10A

Maimonides Mishneh Torah, Hilchot Avodat Kochavim 1:1

בימי אנוש טעו בני האדם טעות גדול ונבערה עצת חכמי אותו
הדור ואנוש עצמו מן הטועים היה, וזו היתה טעותם, אמרו הואיל
והאלהים ברא כוכבים אלו וגלגלים להנהיג את העולם ונתנם
במרום וחלק להם כבוד והם שמשים המשמשים לפניו ראויין הם
לשבחם ולפארם ולחלוק להם כבוד, וזהו רצון האל ברוך הוא לגדל
ולכבד מי שגדלו וכבדו, כמו שהמלך רוצה לכבד העומדים לפניו
וזהו כבודו של מלך, כיון שעלה דבר זה על לבם התחילו לבנות
לכוכבים היכלות ולהקריב להן קרבנות ולשבחם ולפארם בדברים
ולהשתחוות למולם כדי להשיג רצון הבורא בדעתם הרעה, וזה היה
עיקר עבודת כוכבים, וכך היו אומרים עובדיה היודעים עיקרה, לא
שהן אומרים שאין שם אלוה אלא אלא כוכב זה.

During the times of Enosh, mankind made a great mistake, and the wise men of that generation gave thoughtless counsel. Enosh himself was one of those who erred. Their mistake was as follows: They said G-d created stars and spheres to control the world. He placed them on high and treated them with honor, making them servants who minister before Him. Accordingly, it is fitting to praise and glorify them and to treat them with honor. [They perceived] this to be the will of G-d, blessed be He, that they magnify and honor those whom He magnified and honored, just as a king desires that the servants who stand before him be honored. Indeed, doing so is an expression of honor to the king. After conceiving this notion, they began to construct temples to the stars and offer sacrifices to them. They would praise and glorify them with words, and prostrate themselves before them, because by doing so, they would—according to their false conception—be fulfilling the will of G-d. This was the essence of the worship of false gods, and this was the rationale of those who worshiped them. They would not say that there is no other god except for this star.

TEXT 10B

Ibid.

ואחר שארכו הימים עמדו בבני האדם נביאי שקר ואמרו שהאל צוה ואמר להם עבדו כוכב פלוני או כל הכוכבים והקריבו לו ונסכו לו כך וכך ובנו לו היכל ועשו צורתו כדי להשתחוות לו כל העם הנשים והקטנים ושאר עמי הארץ, ומודיע להם צורה שבדה מלבו ואומר זו היא צורת הכוכב פלוני שהודיעוהו בנבואתו, והתחילו על דרך זו לעשות צורות בהיכלות ותחת האילנות ובראשי ההרים ועל הגבעות ומתקבצין ומשתחוים להם ואומרים לכל העם שזו הצורה מטיבה ומריעה וראוי לעובדה וליראה ממנה.

After many years passed, there arose people—false prophets—who told [their nations] that G-d had commanded them to say: Serve this star—or all the stars—sacrifice to it, offer libations to it, build a temple for it, and make an image of it so that all people… could bow to it. He would inform them of a form that he had conceived, and tell them that this is the image of the particular star, claiming that this was revealed to him in a prophetic vision. In this manner, the people began to make images in temples, under trees, and on the tops of mountains and hills. People would gather together and bow down to them and the [false prophets] would say: This image is the source of benefit or harm. It is appropriate to serve it and fear it.

It's All About Me

TEXT 11

The Lubavitcher Rebbe, Likutei Sichot vol. 1, p. 183

נמצא אז די סיבה וואס זיי האבן געדינט עבודה זרה איז געווען בכדי צו האבן, לויט זייער פאלשן באגריף, פון זיי השפעות גשמיות, דאס הייסט צולים זייערע אייגענע פניות.

They served idols because, according to their false understanding, it would bring them physical bounty. In other words, for selfish reasons.

Two Types of Idolaters

TEXT 12

Ibid, p. 185

אן עובד עבודה זרה, אויב רוחניות רירט אים אם, איז בשעת ער
כאפט זיך זיין טעות, וועט ער תשובה טאן. דאקעגן הפוסח כו',
וויבאלד אים איז ניט נוגע דער ענין הרוחניות. אים איז נוגע נאר
זיינע גשמיות, און אפילו קומענדיק צום אמת אז גשמיות העענגט
אפ נאר פון אויבערשטן, וועט ער אויך ניט תשובה טאן צום
אויבערשטן באמת—נאר צוליב די גשמיות.

*If spirituality is at all important to him, an idolater
will repent once he recognizes his error. But one who
"jumps between the two ideas" doesn't care for spirituality at all. He cares only for the physical, and even
upon realizing that the physical depends on G-d alone
he will not sincerely repent—his repentance will only
be for the physical.*

Modern-Day Straddlers

TEXT 13

Ibid, p. 185-186

עס זיינען פאראן אזעלכע וואס צוליב גשמיות׳דיקע פניות, פרנסה,
כבוד המדומה און מה יאמרו הבריות, זיינען זיי מוותר לפי שעה
אויף כמה וכמה ענינים פון תורה ומצות. אויף די פאר טעג צי די
פאר וואכן שטעלט ער אוועק דעם שולחן ערוך צוזאמען מיטן
אויבערשטן כביכול אויפן פאליצע—שעלוו—בכדי מען זאל
ניט זאגן אויף אים אז ער איז א בטלן, אז ער פארשטייט ניט די
היינטיקע צייט...מען דארף זיך פירן א ביסל לויטן רוח הזמן וכו׳.
און צוליב דעם... איז ביי אים רעכט צו פארקויפן, לפי שעה על כל
פנים, דעם אויבערשטן כביכול מיט זיין אייגענע נשמה.

Some people, for the sake of money or perceived prestige and social standing, temporarily give up matters of Torah and mitzvot. For a few days or weeks, such a person leaves the Shulchan Aruch and G-d, so to speak, on the shelf, so that nobody will call him a batlan, *or think he doesn't understand modern times...because today we've got to adopt a modern mindset, etc. For this... he deems it worthwhile to sell, temporarily at least, G-d, so to speak, and his own soul.*

The Straddler's Problem

TEXT 14

Ibid.

דער וואס דינט עבודה זרה רחמנא ליצלן וועט זיך קיין איד פון אים
ניט אפלערנען. וויסנדיק אז ער איז א כופר, האט מיט אים קיינער
ניט קיין געשעפטן. דאקעגן דער פוסח על שתי הסעיפים, וויבאלד
ער איז דאך א מאמין אויך, איז ער בכלל מחטיא את הרבים,
והמחטיא את הרבים קשה מכולם.

No one will take an example from a person who serves idols, G-d forbid. Knowing he rejects G-d altogether, nobody will want to have anything to do with him. But one who "jumps between the two ideas," who is also a believer in G-d—he causes others to sin. And causing others to sin is the most severe of all.

SHOFTIM

Bearing Witness

Working as G-d's Agent

Dedicated in honor of our dear colleague and Founding Director of Torah Studies,
Rabbi Meir Hecht. *May he and his family merit to witness the fulfillment of continuous blessings for health, happiness, nachas and success in all their endeavors.*

PARASHAH OVERVIEW
Shoftim

Moses instructs the people of Israel to appoint judges and law enforcement officers in every city. "Justice, justice shall you pursue," he commands them, and you must administer it without corruption or favoritism. Crimes must be meticulously investigated and evidence thoroughly examined—a minimum of two credible witnesses is required for conviction and punishment.

In every generation, says Moses, there will be those entrusted with the task of interpreting and applying the laws of the Torah. "According to the law that they will teach you, and the judgment they will instruct you, you shall do; you shall not turn away from the thing that they say to you, to the right nor to the left."

Shoftim also includes the prohibitions against idolatry *and* sorcery; *laws governing the appointment and behavior of a* king; *and guidelines for the creation of* "cities of refuge" *for the* inadvertent murderer. *Also set forth are many of the rules of* war: *the exemption from battle for one who has just built a* home, planted a vineyard, married, *or is "afraid and soft-hearted"; the requirement to offer* terms of peace *before attacking a city; and the prohibition against wanton* destruction *of something of value, exemplified by the law that forbids to cut down a* fruit tree *when laying siege (in this context the Torah makes the famous statement,* "For man is a tree of the field"*).*

The Parshah concludes with the law of the eglah arufah—*the special procedure to be followed when a person is killed by an unknown murderer and his body is found in a field—which underscores the* responsibility *of the community and its leaders not only for what they do, but also for what they might have prevented from being done.*

Two Types of Witnesses

Partners in Marriage

TEXT 1

Maimonides, Laws of Marriage, 4:6

Rabbi Moshe ben Maimon
(Maimonides, Rambam)
1135–1204
Halachist, philosopher, author, and physician. Maimonides was born in Cordoba, Spain. After the conquest of Cordoba by the Almohads, he fled Spain and eventually settled in Cairo, Egypt. There, he became the leader of the Jewish community and served as court physician to the vizier of Egypt. He is most noted for authoring the *Mishneh Torah*, an encyclopedic arrangement of Jewish law, and for his philosophical work, *Guide for the Perplexed*. His rulings on Jewish law are integral to the formation of halachic consensus.

המקדש בעד אחד אין חוששין לקידושיו, ואע"פ ששניהם מודין, קל וחומר למקדש בלא עדים.

One who sanctifies a woman for marriage with only one witness, we do not consider at all betrothed, even if both husband and wife agree they were betrothed. All the more so if one performs the marriage with no witnesses at all!

Borrowed Clarity

TEXT 2

Maimonides, Laws of Lender and Borrower, 2:7

אסור לאדם להלוות מעותיו בלא עדים ואפילו לתלמיד חכם
אלא אם כן הלוהו על המשכון והמלוה בשטר משובח יתר, וכל
המלוה בלא עדים עובר משום ולפני עור לא תתן מכשול וגורם
קללה לעצמו.

It is forbidden for one to lend money, even to a trusted Torah scholar, without witnesses. The exceptions are if the lender takes collateral, or, even better, if he takes a promissory note. Whoever lends without witnesses transgresses the law, as the verse states, "Do not place a stumbling block before the blind," and brings a curse upon himself.

To Establish and to Clarify

Rabbi Yosef Rosen
(Rogatchover Ga'on)
1858–1936

One of the prominent talmudic
scholars of the early 20th
century. Born in Rogachev,
Belarus, to a Chasidic family,
his unusual capabilities were
recognized at a young age.
At thirteen he was brought
to Slutsk to study with Rabbi
Yosef Ber Soloveitchik. He
remained there for a full year,
studying primarily with the
rabbi's son, the legendary
Chaim Soloveitchik. Later, he
moved on to Shklov, where
he studied with Rabbi Moshe
Yehoshua Leib Diskin. After
a period in Warsaw, the home
city of his wife, he assumed
the rabbinate of the Chasidic
community in Dvinsk, Latvia.

His works, titled *Tsafnat
Pane'ach*, are famed for both
their depth and difficulty.

TEXT 3

Rabbi Yosef Rosen of Rogachov, The Rogachover Gaon,
Tzafnat Panei'ach, ch. 13, 10:3

מיני עדות . . שהדבר נעשה על ידי זה, כמו עדי קידושין וגיטין . .
עדי ממון זה עדי בירור.

*The types of testimony…include the type through
which a thing is* performed, *such as marriage or divorce testimony…as opposed to monetary witnesses,
who serve merely as* clarifying *witnesses.*

Two Sides of One Word

TEXT 4

Devarim (Deuteronomy) 19:15

לֹא יָקוּם עֵד אֶחָד בְּאִישׁ לְכָל עָוֹן וּלְכָל חַטָּאת בְּכָל חֵטְא אֲשֶׁר יֶחֱטָא
עַל פִּי שְׁנֵי עֵדִים אוֹ עַל פִּי שְׁלֹשָׁה עֵדִים יָקוּם דָּבָר:

*A single witness cannot establish incrimination for any
sin or any fraud. A sin can only be established by two
or three witnesses.*

To Reveal a Secret

Whom G-d Calls to the Stand

TEXT 5

Devarim (Deuteronomy) 30:19

הַעִידֹתִי בָכֶם הַיּוֹם אֶת הַשָּׁמַיִם וְאֶת הָאָרֶץ הַחַיִּים וְהַמָּוֶת נָתַתִּי לְפָנֶיךָ הַבְּרָכָה וְהַקְּלָלָה וּבָחַרְתָּ בַּחַיִּים לְמַעַן תִּחְיֶה אַתָּה וְזַרְעֶךָ:

I am calling upon heaven and earth to testify against you. I have set in front of you life and death, blessing and curse, and you should choose life, so you and your children will live.

TEXT 6

Yeshaya (Isaiah) 43:10-12

אַתֶּם עֵדַי נְאֻם ה' וְעַבְדִּי אֲשֶׁר בָּחָרְתִּי לְמַעַן תֵּדְעוּ וְתַאֲמִינוּ לִי וְתָבִינוּ כִּי אֲנִי הוּא לְפָנַי לֹא נוֹצַר אֵ-ל וְאַחֲרַי לֹא יִהְיֶה: אָנֹכִי אָנֹכִי ה' וְאֵין מִבַּלְעָדַי מוֹשִׁיעַ: אָנֹכִי הִגַּדְתִּי וְהוֹשַׁעְתִּי וְהִשְׁמַעְתִּי וְאֵין בָּכֶם זָר וְאַתֶּם עֵדַי נְאֻם ה' וַאֲנִי אֵ-ל:

"You are my witnesses," says G-d, "and My servant that I've chosen, in order that you might know, and believe in Me, and understand that I am He; before Me no god was formed and after Me none will exist.

"I, I am G-d, and aside from Me there is no savior.

"I spoke of it, and redeemed, and made it known, and there is no foreign god among you. You are My witnesses," says G-d, "and I am G-d."

TEXT 7

Zohar vol. 3, 86a

Zohar
The seminal work of Kabbalah, Jewish mysticism. The Zohar is a mystical commentary on the Torah, written in Aramaic and Hebrew. According to Arizal, the Zohar contains the teachings of Rabbi Shimon bar Yocha'i who lived in the Land of Israel during the 2nd century. The Zohar has become one of the indispensable texts of traditional Judaism, alongside and nearly equal in stature to the Mishnah and Talmud.

פתח רבי אלעזר ואמר "אתם עדי נאם ה' ועבדי אשר בחרתי למען תדעו ותאמינו וגו'". אתם עדי—אלין אינון ישראל.

Rabbi Elazar opened and said: The verse states, "'You are My witnesses,' says G-d, 'and My servant I have chosen in order that you might know, and believe in Me,' etc." To whom does the phrase "you are My witnesses" refer?

To the people of Israel.

114   *Torah Studies* Season Four 5777

Revealing the Hidden

TEXT 8

Rabbi Shneur Zalman of Liadi, Likkutei Torah, Pekudei, p. 4a

נקראו גם כן נשמות ישראל שבטי י-ה עדות לישראל. כי הנה על
דרך משל ענין עדות ועדים שהיא הגדה הנאמנת אין שייך אלא על
דבר הנסתר ונעלם מעיני הכל על זה צריך עדות שיעידו על זה אבל
על דבר הנגלה אין צריך ואין שייך עדות. ואפילו על מלתא דעבידא
לאגלויי ממש מיד לא הצריכה התורה עדות. כמו כן על דרך משל
פירוש עדות לישראל זהו על...בחינת י-ה הנקרא עלמא דאתכסיא.
כי... ענין אור הנמשך בכלים זהו הנקרא עלמא דאתגליא... הוא
מקור לבי"ע והוא בסדר ההשתלשלות ואין שייך על זה עדות.
אבל... עלמא דאתכסיא שהוא למעלה מסדר ההשתלשלות ואינו
נתפס כלל בשום כלי כו' כי לית מחשבה תפיסא ביה כלל, ולכן על
המשכת בחינת זו נאמר שבטי י-ה עדות לישראל שעם היות שאין
מושג המהות ממש, יש עדות על זה.

Rabbi Shneur Zalman of Liadi (Alter Rebbe) 1745–1812 Chasidic rebbe, halachic authority, and founder of the Chabad movement. The Alter Rebbe was born in Liozna, Belarus, and was among the principal students of the Magid of Mezeritch. His numerous works include the *Tanya*, an early classic containing the fundamentals of Chabad Chasidism, and *Shulchan Aruch HaRav*, an expanded and reworked code of Jewish law.

The souls of Israel are called "tribes of G-d, witnesses of Israel." ...They are metaphorical witnesses, for what are witnesses and testimony? —a trusted pronouncement relevant only to what is hidden and concealed from the public. For something that is revealed, testimony is not necessary and is not relevant. Even if it's something not yet known, but can immediately be learned by the public, also doesn't require testimony...

With regard to the G-dly energy that is invested within the worldly reality, dubbed the "revealed words," the energy is considered to be integrated within the perceivable realm, and thus, the term "testimony" is irrelevant. Then, there are "hidden worlds" that are beyond the perceivable realm. They are not integrated into any specific form of expression inasmuch as they completely transcend all sense of integration. It is regarding these worlds the term "testimony" is used, "testimony of Israel." Though one cannot possibly perceive these matters on their face, it is possible to "testify" about them.

The Revealed Truth of G-d

TEXT 9

Iyov (Job), 19:26

וְאַחַר עוֹרִי נִקְּפוּ זֹאת וּמִבְּשָׂרִי אֶחֱזֶה אֱלוֹקַּ׃

And after my skin, they have cut into this, and from my flesh I see G-d.

The Infinite Secret

TEXT 10

Rabbi Menachem Mendel Schneersohn of Lubavitch,
The Tzemach Tzedek, Sefer HaChakirah, p.101b

היינו מה שאנו רואים בנבראים, השמים והארץ וכל צבאם, יש
הארה והשפעה מכח האין סוף דוקא, אף שהנבראים בעצם הם
בעלי גבול והיינו מה דכח ההשפעה שבנבראים הנ"ל
היא בלי שיעור וגבול כלל שהרי שיתא אלפי שני דהוי עלמא לא
נפסקה עדיין אור השפע האלקי להוות מאין ליש... הגם שהשפע
באה בבחינת מספר וגבול, היינו שהוא מוציאם במספר אבל כח
השופע בהם הוא בחינת אין סוף, שהרי אין לה הפסק...
ונמצא שהשפעה זו האלקית הגם שבאה בבחינת מספר, עם כל זה
ניכר ונראה בנביעתה בלי הפסק שבאה מכח השופע של אין סוף
ברוך הוא.

Rabbi Menachem Mendel Schneersohn of Lubavitch (*Tzemach Tzedek*) 1789–1866

Chasidic rebbe and noted author. The *Tzemach Tzedek* was the third leader of the Chabad Chasidic movement and a noted authority on Jewish law. His numerous works include halachic responsa, Chasidic discourses, and Kabbalistic writings. Active in the plight of Russian Jewry, he worked to alleviate the plight of the Cantonists, Jewish children kidnapped to serve in the Czar's army. He passed away in Lubavitch, leaving seven sons and two daughters.

All of Creation—the heaven and the earth and all their hosts—are animated by an infinite energy of G-d. Though the created matter may be indeed limited and finite, the fact remains that there is a consistent, eternal stream of energy from G-d. After all, G-d has not stopped animating the world for six thousand years… While it is true that the energy integrates into something finite and limited, it doesn't change the fact that the energy behind it is infinite, inasmuch that it never ceases to create…

It emerges that though the G-dly energy that flows into this world is finite and limited, the consistent, ceaseless stream of life demonstrates that it stems from G-d's infinite light, may it be blessed.

To Make It Real

The Spiritual Establishing Witness

TEXT 11A

The Lubavitcher Rebbe, Reshimot, Booklet 160

> לגדולות מזה נוצר עם ישראל . . ישראל במעשיהם אינם רק
> מפרסמים אלקותו בעולם, אלא לוקחים גם חלק פעיל בכל מעשה
> בראשית—שעושים הגשמיות כלי לאלקות.

The people of Israel were crafted with an important mission... With his or her actions, a Jew does not merely publicize *G-d's presence in this world, rather he or she takes an* active *role in the process of Creation; the Jew* makes *the world a* conduit *for G-dliness.*

Rabbi Menachem Mendel Schneerson
1902–1994
The towering Jewish leader of the 20th century, known as "the Lubavitcher Rebbe," or simply as "the Rebbe." Born in southern Ukraine, the Rebbe escaped Nazi-occupied Europe, arriving in the U.S. in June 1941. The Rebbe inspired and guided the revival of traditional Judaism after the European devastation, impacting virtually every Jewish community the world over. The Rebbe often emphasized that the performance of just one additional good deed could usher in the era of Mashiach. The Rebbe's scholarly talks and writings have been printed in more than 200 volumes.

Holy Matrimony

TEXT 11B

Ibid.

> החתונה היותר גדולה של אלקות וכל הבריאה, ובני ישראל הם
> העדים שעושים חלקי מהקידושין, ולא רק לברר הדבה.

The greatest wedding that can be is the marriage of G-d and all of Creation. The Jewish people are the witnesses who play an active role in establishing the marriage—they do not only clarify.

An Active Guarantor

TEXT 11C

Ibid.

ומוסר השכל בחיי כל אחד.

יש שיטה שיסתפק בד' אמות שלו שמתנהג על פי התורה והמצוות, ואינו פעיל במה שחוץ מזה.

ולא זהו דרישת שיטת החסידות—כי אמרו רז"ל "כל ישראל ערבים זה בזה", והסיסמא אהבת ישראל, ולהתעניין בכל ענייניו באופן פעיל, היינו ענין עצמי, שבכל הוייתו הוא עושה וממשיך אלקות בעולם.

And the lesson in each of our lives:

There is a school of thought that thinks it is sufficient for a Jew to conduct his or her personal life according to Torah values, but does not engage or influence that which exists beyond.

This is not what the Chassidic way demands of us. Our Sages state, "All Israel are responsible for one another." Our "slogan" is "Love a fellow Jew"—to take an active interest in all *matters of another Jew. A Jew ought to conduct him or herself in a way that is contagious— everything they do spreads G-dliness within the world.*

7

KI TEITZEI

The Divorce Dilemma

A Deep Dive into the Divorce Dynamic

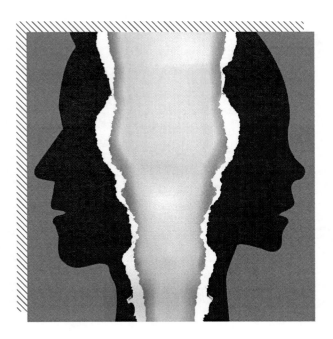

*Dedicated in honor of the birthday of our friend **Rabbi Shraga Sherman**, 8 Elul.*
May he and his family merit to witness the fulfillment of continuous blessings
for health, happiness, nachas and success in all their endeavors.

PARASHAH OVERVIEW
Ki Teitzei

Seventy-four of the Torah's 613 commandments (mitzvot) are in the parashah of Ki Teitzei. These include the laws of the beautiful captive, the inheritance rights of the firstborn, the wayward and rebellious son, burial and dignity of the dead, returning a lost object, sending away the mother bird before taking her young, the duty to erect a safety fence around the roof of one's home, and the various forms of kilayim (forbidden plant and animal hybrids).

Also recounted are the judicial procedures and penalties for adultery, for the rape or seduction of an unmarried girl, and for a husband who falsely accuses his wife of infidelity. The following cannot marry a person of Jewish lineage: a mamzer (someone born from an adulterous or incestuous relationship); a male of Moabite or Ammonite descent; a first- or second-generation Edomite or Egyptian.

Our Parshah also includes laws governing the purity of the military camp; the prohibition against turning in an escaped slave; the duty to pay a worker on time, and to allow anyone working for you—man or animal—to "eat on the job"; the proper treatment of a debtor, and the prohibition against charging interest on a loan; the laws of divorce (from which are also derived many of the laws of marriage); the penalty of thirty-nine lashes for transgression of a Torah prohibition; and the procedures for yibbum ("levirate marriage") of the wife of a deceased childless brother, or chalitzah ("removing of the shoe") in the case that the brother-in-law does not wish to marry her.

Ki Teitzei concludes with the obligation to remember "what Amalek did to you on the road, on your way out of Egypt."

Introduction

TEXT 1

Talmud Tractate Gitin 90b

Babylonian Talmud
A literary work of monumental proportions that draws upon the legal, spiritual, intellectual, ethical, and historical traditions of Judaism. The 37 tractates of the Babylonian Talmud contain the teachings of the Jewish sages from the period after the destruction of the 2nd Temple through the 5th century CE. It has served as the primary vehicle for the transmission of the Oral Law and the education of Jews over the centuries; it is the entry point for all subsequent legal, ethical, and theological Jewish scholarship.

כל המגרש את אשתו ראשונה, אפילו מזבח מוריד עליו דמעות, שנאמר " . . . כסות דמעה את מזבח ה' בכי ואנקה, מאין עוד פנות אל המנחה ולקחת רצון מידכם". וכתיב "ואמרתם, 'על מה?' על כי ה' העיד בינך ובין אשת נעוריך אשר אתה בגדתה בה, והיא חברתך ואשת בריתך".

When one divorces the wife of his youth, the altar sheds tears, as it is written, ". . . You cover the altar of G-d with tears, weeping, and sighing; He no longer pays attention to your offering, nor receives it graciously from your hand." The [following] verse continues: "'Why is this?' you ask. Because G-d is witness between you and the wife of your youth—your companion, the woman with whom you entered a covenant—whom you have betrayed."

Marriage in the Torah

TEXT 2

Devarim (Deuteronomy) 24:1-2

כִּי יִקַּח אִישׁ אִשָּׁה וּבְעָלָהּ וְהָיָה אִם לֹא תִמְצָא חֵן בְּעֵינָיו כִּי מָצָא בָהּ
עֶרְוַת דָּבָר וְכָתַב לָהּ סֵפֶר כְּרִיתֻת וְנָתַן בְּיָדָהּ וְשִׁלְּחָהּ מִבֵּיתוֹ:
וְיָצְאָה מִבֵּיתוֹ וְהָלְכָה וְהָיְתָה לְאִישׁ אַחֵר:

When a man takes a wife and is intimate with her, and it happens that she does not find favor in his eyes because he discovers in her an unseemly [moral] matter, and he writes for her a bill of divorce and places it into her hand, and sends her away from his house.

And she leaves his house and goes and marries another man.

Open-Door Policy

TEXT 3

Rabbi Yosef ben Arzah, Yosef Da'at to Tractate Gittin

ועל דרך המליצה נאמר, שאומרים לו לאדם לפני שנושא אשה: לעולם הדלת פתוחה לפניך להתנתק מקשר זה, ואין חירותך ניטלת ממך על ידו. ידיעה מקדימה זו כשלעצמה מהווה תנאי ובסיס מוקדם ליציבותם של הקדושין וקיומם.

Homiletically, it can be said that [this Scriptural anomaly of marriage in the context of divorce] conveys a message to the prospective bride and groom: There is always an open door to absolve this relationship, and your freedom is not forever taken from you. This very knowledge actually helps assure the stability and lasting chance of the marriage.

Serious Commitment

"Doesn't Find Favor"

TEXT 4

Talmud Tractate Gitin, 90a

בית שמאי אומרים, לא יגרש אדם את אשתו אלא אם כן מצא בה
דבר ערוה, שנאמר "כי מצא בה ערות דבר".
ובית הלל אומרים, אפילו הקדיחה תבשילו, שנאמר, "כי מצא בה
ערות דבר".
רבי עקיבא אומר, אפילו מצא אחרת נאה הימנה, שנאמר, "והיה אם
לא תמצא חן בעיניו".

The School of Shamai taught: A man ought not to divorce his wife unless she is guilty of immoral misconduct, as it is stated, "Because he discovers in her an immoral matter."

The School of Hillel taught: [A man may divorce his wife] even if she burned his dish, as it is stated, "Because he discovers in her an immoral [act, or any other malicious] matter."

Rabbi Akiva says: [A man may divorce his wife] even if he found another more attractive than she, as it is stated, "And it happens that she does not find favor in his eyes."

The Case for Divorce

TEXT 5

Rabbi Yisroel Lipschitz, Tiferet Yisroel to Mishnah Gittin 9:10

> "אפילו הקדיחה תבשילו". ששרפה תבשילו והתכוונה להקניטתו.

"Even if she burned his dish." That is, in an instance when she intentionally burned it to provoke him.

TEXT 6

Talmud Tractate Ketubot, 72a

> אין אדם דר עם נחש בכפיפה.

A person cannot live together with a snake in one basket.

TEXT 7

Rabbi Don Yitzchak Abarbanel, Abarbanel to Devarim 24:1

האמנם כל התועלות האלה לא ימצאו ולא ימשכו בחברת האדם
עם אשתו, כי אם בהיותם מסכימים בטבע ובמזג, כפי מה שאפשר,
אשר זה יביא ביניהם האהבה וההסכמה....

ומפני זה צוה יתעלה, שכאשר האדם לא יסכים מזגו וטבעו לטבע
אשתו, כי זה הוא "והיה אם לא תמצא חן בעיניו כי מצא בה ערות
דבר", שחלוף מזגיהם תסבב הסבה, שאז יגרשנה—שמוטב לגרשה,
משתרבה השנאה והריב והקטטה ביניהם...

האמנם, אם כבר באו להנשא, ולא יבאו בהסכמה והאותות בשום
צד, בחרה התורה שיגרשנה, כי בחירת הרע במיעוטו. ואולי ישא
אחרת דומה לטבעו ומזגו, והיא תנשא לאחר הדומה לה, ולא יחיו
כל ימיהם חיי צער, ואולי יבאו לשפיכות דמים, וגלוי עריות.

**Rabbi Don Yitzchak
Abarbanel**
1437–1508

Biblical exegete and
statesman. Abarbanel was
born in Lisbon, Portugal,
and served as a minister in
the court of King Alfonso V
of Portugal. After intrigues
at court led to accusations
against him, he fled to Spain,
where he once again served
as a counselor to royalty. It
is claimed that Abarbanel
offered King Ferdinand and
Queen Isabella large sums
of money for the revocation
of their Edict of Expulsion of
1492, but to no avail. After
the expulsion, he eventually
settled in Italy where he wrote
a commentary on Scripture, as
well as other venerated works.

A man and woman will only experience the advantages and qualities of marriage if they are compatible in nature and character, as much as possible. Such synchronism will bring harmony and love…

For this reason, G-d commanded that when a man and woman are no longer compatible—the meaning of the words, "she does not find favor in his eyes for he found an immoral thing"—in such an instance, it is best to divorce. Better to divorce than to let tension and discord continue to develop…

If they are already married and, for whatever reason, they cannot come to any agreement, the Torah chooses the option of divorce, for it is the lesser of the two evils.

Who knows?—maybe this one will marry another person more compatible with him, and this one will marry another person more compatible with her. Better that than living an entire life in misery, possibly leading to horrible things like murder and lechery.

Free to Stay

TEXT 8

Zohar vol. 1, 49b

Zohar

The seminal work of Kabbalah, Jewish mysticism. The Zohar is a mystical commentary on the Torah, written in Aramaic and Hebrew. According to Arizal, the Zohar contains the teachings of Rabbi Shimon bar Yocha'i who lived in the Land of Israel during the second century. The Zohar has become one of the indispensable texts of traditional Judaism, alongside and nearly equal in stature to the Mishnah and Talmud.

השתא שרי לשבחא לה: "'לזאת יקרא אשה'—דא היא דלא
ישתכח כוותיה, דא היא יקרא דביתא, כלהון נשין גבה ככופא בפני
בני נשא. אבל לזאת יקרא אשה, שלימו דכלא, לזאת ולא לאחרא".

Adam began to sing Eve's praises, "'This shall be called woman'—this is the peerless one; this is the pride of the house, who surpasses all other women as a human being surpasses an ape. This one is perfect in all points, and she alone merits the title of woman."

TEXT 9

Rabbi Avraham Eliyahu Kitov, Ish Ubeito, pp. 62–68

Rabbi Eliyahu Kitov
1912–1976
Polish-born Israeli educator and community activist. He helped establish the Agudat Yisrael Workers party. In 1954 he left the political scene, dedicating the later years of his life to writing. His most noted works, *Sefer Hatoda'ah* (*The Book of our Heritage*), and *Ish Ubeito* (*The Jew and His Home*), are considered essential works on Jewish practice and belief.

שמא תאמר עשוי הוא היתר הגירושין לרופף את ברית הנשואין ולהפריד בין הדבקים ולהטיל מוראו בכל שעת קטטה ומריבה שבין איש לאשתו?

אין הדבר כן, אלא היתר הגירושין בישראל חיזוק גדול הוא לברית הנשואין, שהוא עושה את הדבק ביניהם שיהא דבק טוב מרצון ולא מאונס . . .

כל נתיבותיה שלום—אפילו זה שדומה בעיניך כאילו יש בה פירוד. אף משפט הגט לא ניתן אלא לשלום הבריות ולמען שלמות המשפחה . . .

רק הסר נא דאגה זו מלבם והשב להם שלוותם, לידע כי חרותם לא נטלה מהם מכל וכל . . . לא יאבדו עולמם בשעה אחת של חרון אף אלא ישבו בשלוה ויצפו לזעם שיעבור. נמצא שאפילו בשעה שאהבתם פגומה—חייהם חיי רצון ולא חיי אונס וזעם. מה הוא הדבר שמרגיעם בשעת כעסם? הווה אומר: דבר זה שאמרו חכמים: אפילו מצא אחרת נאה הימנה רשאי הוא לגרשה! משל, למה הדבר דומה? לאחד שהמלכות גזרה עליו שישב כלוא בביתו. עדיין לא עבר עליו יום אחד בכלאו והריהו יושב בביתו ומצטער. שמא תאמר אדם זה קשה לו ישיבתו בתוך ביתו? והרי כמה וכמה פעמים שראינוהו מסתגר בתוך ביתו וישב בו להנאתו ימים אחדים ומתענג בו. אמור מעתה: לא ביתו גורם לצערו אלא הגזירה גורמת; נוטל אתה את הגזירה, הרי הוא יושב במקומו ומתענג.

One might think that the permission to divorce weakens the marriage institution, for the fear of divorce will loom large whenever the husband and wife quarrel or fight. This is not so.

Paradoxically, the permission to divorce strengthens marriage; it makes for a beautiful union—a union that stands upon the free will of its parties, not coercion. . . .

"All the [Torah's] pathways are peaceful." Even the law of divorce, which is seemingly intended to create separation, is actually intended to engender peace and preserve the integrity of the family unit. . . .

[The Torah] removes the worry from the heart and restores people's serenity, for they are assured in the knowledge that their freedom has not at all been taken from them. . . Hence, they will not destroy their lives in a fit of anger; rather, they will remain at peace and wait out the stressful moments in marriage. What calms them in their moments of anger? That which the Sages said: "Even if he finds another more beautiful than she, he may divorce her."

This is like a person placed under house arrest. One day of his incarceration has yet to pass, and there he is, sitting in his home, completely miserable. Is it because he finds staying in his home unbearable? That cannot be so, because on many previous occasions he was observed not leaving his home for several days at a time, and he enjoyed and relished that private time! It is clear that it is not staying at home that is so distressing to him, but being coerced to do so. In the absence of the coercion, he would happily sit in his home.

A Cosmic Rift

Marriage's Cosmic Implications

TEXT 10

Avot DeRabbi Natan 28:3

כל המשים שלום בתוך ביתו, מעלה עליו הכתוב כאילו משים
שלום בישראל על כל אחד ואחד.
וכל המטיל קנאה ותחרות בתוך ביתו, מעלה עליו הכתוב כאילו
מטיל קנאה ותחרות בישראל.

*G-d considers those who bring peace to their homes as
if they brought peace to the entire nation of Israel and
to every single individual.*

*G-d considers those who create strife and enmity in
their homes as if they created strife and enmity among
the entire nation of Israel.*

Avot DeRabbi Natan

A commentary on, and an
elaboration of, the mishnaic
tractate Avot, bearing the
name of Rabbi Natan, one
of the sages of the Mishnah.
The work exists in two
very different versions, one
of which appears in many
editions of the Talmud.

Ushering Global Redemption

TEXT 11

Text of Sheva Berachot

ברוך אתה ה׳ . . . אשר ברא ששון ושמחה, חתן וכלה. גילה, רנה,
דיצה, וחדוה, אהבה, ואחוה, שלום, ורעות. מהרה ה׳ אלקינו ישמע
בערי יהודה ובחוצות ירושלים. קול ששון וקול שמחה, קול חתן
וקול כלה, קול מצהלות חתנים מחפתם ונערים ממשתה נגינתם.

Blessed are You, G-d . . . Who created joy and happiness; groom and bride; gladness, jubilation, cheer, and delight; love, friendship, harmony, and fellowship. O G-d, let there speedily be heard in the streets of Jerusalem the sound of joy and the sound of happiness, the sound of a groom and the sound of a bride, the sound of exultation of grooms from under their wedding canopies and youths from their joyous banquets.

TEXT 12

Talmud Tractate Yoma, 9b

מקדש שני, שהיו עוסקין בתורה ובמצות וגמילות חסדים מפני מה
חרב? מפני שהיתה בו שנאת חנם.

If the Jews were engaged in Torah and good deeds, why was the Second Temple destroyed? Because of baseless hatred.

Our Marriage with G-d

TEXT 13

Midrash Bamidbar Rabah, 12

ביום חתונתו, זה סיני, חיתונין היו.

[What is the verse referring to when it mentions] the day "G-d got married"? The giving of the Torah at Mt. Sinai. This was a marriage with the Jewish people.

Bamidbar Rabah

An exegetical commentary on the first seven chapters of the book of Numbers and a homiletic commentary on the rest of the book. The first part of *Bamidbar Rabah* is notable for its inclusion of esoteric material; the second half is essentially identical to *Midrash Tanchuma* on the book of Numbers. It was first printed in Constantinople in 1512, together with four other midrashic works on the other four books of the Pentateuch.

TEXT 14

Rabbi Shneur Zalman of Liadi, Likutei Torah, 1a

**Rabbi Shneur
Zalman of Liadi**
(Alter Rebbe)
1745–1812

Chasidic rebbe, halachic
authority, and founder of
the Chabad movement. The
Alter Rebbe was born in
Liozna, Belarus, and was
among the principal students
of the Magid of Mezeritch.
His numerous works include
the *Tanya*, an early classic
containing the fundamentals
of Chabad Chasidism, and
Shulchan Aruch HaRav,
an expanded and reworked
code of Jewish law.

"שיר השירים אשר לשלמה ישקני מנשיקות פיהו כי טובים דודיך מיין".

הנה נודע שהקדוש ברוך הוא נקרא חתן. וכנסת ישראל נקרא בשם כלה. והיינו על שם המשכת והשפעת התורה לישראל. וכמאמר רז"ל ביום חתונתו זה מתן תורה...

והנה כלה יש בו ב' פירושים. הא' מלשון כליון שמכלה ומבלה הכל מלשון כפלפה.... והב' מלשון כלתה נפשי כו' והיינו תשוקת הנפש לידבק וליכלל באורו יתברך.

"The Song of Songs, which is Solomon's. Let him kiss me with the kisses of his mouth, for your love is better than wine."

It is known that G-d is called the groom and the Jews are the bride, namely due to the downward flow of Torah from G-d to the Jews. As our Sages stated, "Matan Torah was G-d's wedding day."…

Now, there are two interpretations for the word "kallah." It can be related to the word "expiration," as in something that is all-consuming… The second interpretation is that it comes from the expression "My souls yearns for G-d." This is the strong desire of the soul to cleave to and be united in the infinite light of G-d.

TEXT 15

Midrash Shemot Rabah, 15:3 1

העולם הזה אירוסין היו . . . אבל לימות המשיח יהיו נישואין,
שנאמר "כי בועליך עושיך".

This world is like a betrothal [period between G-d and Israel]. The wedding will take place in the Messianic era, as it says, "For your Maker will be your husband."

Shemot Rabah

An early rabbinic commentary on the Book of Exodus. Midrash is the designation of a particular genre of rabbinic literature usually forming a running commentary on specific books of the Bible. *Shemot Rabah*, written mostly in Hebrew, provides textual exegeses, expounds upon the biblical narrative, and develops and illustrates moral principles. It was first printed in Constantinople in 1512 together with four other midrashic works on the other four books of the Pentateuch.

TEXT 16

Rabbi Dovber of Mezritch, Maggid Devarav LeYaakov §198

דע מה למעלה ממך פרויש דע כל מה שלמעלה הכל הוא ממך.

[The Mishnah in Avot states,] "Know that which is Above you." An alternative explanation: Know that everything on High is from [i.e., hinged upon] you.

Rabbi Dovber "the Magid" of Mezeritch
d. 1772

Was the primary disciple and eventual successor of the Baal Shem Tov. Amongst his disciples were the founders of various Chasidic dynasties, including Rabbi Nachum of Chernobyl, Rabbi Levi Yitzchak of Berditchev, and Rabbi Shneur Zalman of Liadi. His teachings, recorded by his students, appear in various volumes including the *Magid Devarav Leya'akov.*

Why Is the "Going Getting Tough"?

TEXT 17

Talmud Tractate Sanhedrin, 97a

שית אלפי שני הוו עלמא.

The world will last for six thousand years [after which it will enter the Messianic era].

TEXT 18

The Lubavitcher Rebbe, Igrot Kodesh vol. 4 p. 433

Rabbi Menachem Mendel Schneerson
1902–1994
The towering Jewish leader of the 20th century, known as "the Lubavitcher Rebbe," or simply as "the Rebbe." Born in southern Ukraine, the Rebbe escaped Nazi-occupied Europe, arriving in the U.S. in June 1941. The Rebbe inspired and guided the revival of traditional Judaism after the European devastation, impacting virtually every Jewish community the world over. The Rebbe often emphasized that the performance of just one additional good deed could usher in the era of Mashiach. The Rebbe's scholarly talks and writings have been printed in more than 200 volumes.

ואם בכל עת הפליגו רבותינו זכרונם לברכה במעלת השלום בית, על אחת כמה וכמה בערב שבת קדש. ואנו עתה כולנו בתוך כלל ישראל בערב שבת קדש לאחר חצות, שקרב קץ גלותנו וביאת משיח צדקנו.

מובן שההעלם וההסתר ביותר הוא בנוגע לשלום בית, כי ידוע שגדול השלום וכל התורה כולה דרכיה דרכי נועם וכל נתיבותיה שלום, ובפרט בגלות זה האחרון שכמאמר רבותינו זכרונם לברכה ביומא ט' ע"ב בא בסיבת העדר השלום, וכל כמה שמתקרב קץ הגלות הרי ההתאבקות מצד שכנגד הוא ביותר בנוגע שלא להניח לעשות שלום בעולם בכלל ובין איש ואשתו דלמטה שלהם בדוגמת איש ואשה דלמעלה בפרט.

אבל לפום גמלא שיחנא, ובודאי נותנים הכחות על זה לעמוד בנסיון.

If, at all times, our Sages, of blessed memory, spoke of the extreme importance of preserving marital harmony, how much more so this pertains to the eve of the holy Sabbath. We and our entire nation now stand on the eve of the holy Sabbath after midday, for the end of our exile and the coming of Mashiach is imminent.

Maintaining marital harmony is so challenging because of the great importance of peace—to the extent that regarding the entire Torah it is said, "Its ways are pleasant ways and all its pathways are peaceful." Preserving peace is particularly [important, and thus] challenging in our present exile, which our Sages tell us was caused by a lack of peace.

As we approach the end of this exile, the [unholy forces of the] "other side" exert great effort to ensure that peace does not prevail—in the world at large, and especially between husband and wife, who correspond to the supernal husband and wife [i.e., G-d and Israel].

Nevertheless, "the camel is only loaded with a burden that is in accordance with its strength." Hence, we are certainly provided [by G-d] with the powers necessary to successfully meet this great challenge.

8

KI TAVO

The Gift of the Giver

The Gratitude-Happiness Connection

Dedicated in honor of our dear colleague and member of the Torah Studies editorial board,
Rabbi Levi Fogelman. *May he and his family merit to witness the fulfillment of continuous blessings for health, happiness, nachas and success in all their endeavors.*

PARASHAH OVERVIEW
Ki Tavo

Moses instructs the people of Israel: When you enter the land that G-d is giving to you as your eternal heritage, and you settle it and cultivate it, bring the first-ripened fruits (bikkurim) of your orchard to the Holy Temple, and declare your gratitude for all that G-d has done for you.

Our parashah also includes the laws of the tithes given to the Levites and to the poor, and detailed instructions on how to proclaim the blessings and the curses on Mount Gerizim and Mount Ebal—as discussed in the beginning of the parashah of Re'eh. Moses reminds the people that they are G-d's chosen people, and that they, in turn, have chosen G-d.

The latter part of Ki Tavo consists of the tochachah *("rebuke"). After listing the blessings with which G-d will reward the people when they follow the laws of the Torah, Moses gives a long, harsh account of the bad things—illness, famine, poverty, and exile—that shall befall them if they abandon G-d's commandments.*

Moses concludes by telling the people that only today, forty years after their birth as a people, have they attained "a heart to know, eyes to see, and ears to hear."

The First-Fruit Proclamation

First Fruits

TEXT 1A

Devarim (Deuteronomy) 26:1-4

וְהָיָה כִּי תָבוֹא אֶל הָאָרֶץ אֲשֶׁר ה' אֱלֹקֶיךָ נֹתֵן לְךָ נַחֲלָה וִירִשְׁתָּהּ וְיָשַׁבְתָּ בָּהּ:

וְלָקַחְתָּ מֵרֵאשִׁית כָּל פְּרִי הָאֲדָמָה אֲשֶׁר תָּבִיא מֵאַרְצְךָ אֲשֶׁר ה' אֱלֹקֶיךָ נֹתֵן לָךְ וְשַׂמְתָּ בַטֶּנֶא וְהָלַכְתָּ אֶל הַמָּקוֹם אֲשֶׁר יִבְחַר ה' אֱלֹקֶיךָ לְשַׁכֵּן שְׁמוֹ שָׁם:

וּבָאתָ אֶל הַכֹּהֵן אֲשֶׁר יִהְיֶה בַּיָּמִים הָהֵם וְאָמַרְתָּ אֵלָיו הִגַּדְתִּי הַיּוֹם ה' אֱלֹקֶיךָ כִּי בָאתִי אֶל הָאָרֶץ אֲשֶׁר נִשְׁבַּע ה' לַאֲבֹתֵינוּ לָתֶת לָנוּ:

וְלָקַח הַכֹּהֵן הַטֶּנֶא מִיָּדֶךָ וְהִנִּיחוֹ לִפְנֵי מִזְבַּח ה' אֱלֹקֶיךָ:

And it will be, when you come into the land that the Lord, your G-d, gives you for an inheritance, and you possess it and settle in it,

That you shall take of the first of all the fruit of the ground, which you will bring from your land, which the Lord, your G-d, is giving you. And you shall put [them] into a basket and go to the place that the Lord, your G-d, will choose to have His Name dwell there.

And you shall come to the kohen who will be [serving] in those days, and say to him, "I declare this day to the

Lord, your G-d, that I have come to the land that G-d swore to our forefathers to give us."

And the kohen will take the basket from your hand, laying it before the altar of the Lord, your G-d.

History Run-Down

TEXT 1B

Ibid, 26:5–10

וְעָנִיתָ וְאָמַרְתָּ לִפְנֵי ה' אֱלֹקֶיךָ אֲרַמִּי אֹבֵד אָבִי וַיֵּרֶד מִצְרַיְמָה וַיָּגָר שָׁם
בִּמְתֵי מְעָט וַיְהִי שָׁם לְגוֹי גָּדוֹל עָצוּם וָרָב:
וַיָּרֵעוּ אֹתָנוּ הַמִּצְרִים וַיְעַנּוּנוּ וַיִּתְּנוּ עָלֵינוּ עֲבֹדָה קָשָׁה:
וַנִּצְעַק אֶל ה' אֱלֹקֵי אֲבֹתֵינוּ וַיִּשְׁמַע ה' אֶת קֹלֵנוּ וַיַּרְא אֶת עָנְיֵנוּ וְאֶת
עֲמָלֵנוּ וְאֶת לַחֲצֵנוּ:
וַיּוֹצִאֵנוּ ה' מִמִּצְרַיִם בְּיָד חֲזָקָה וּבִזְרֹעַ נְטוּיָה וּבְמֹרָא גָּדֹל
וּבְאֹתוֹת וּבְמֹפְתִים:
וַיְבִאֵנוּ אֶל הַמָּקוֹם הַזֶּה וַיִּתֶּן לָנוּ אֶת הָאָרֶץ הַזֹּאת אֶרֶץ זָבַת חָלָב וּדְבָשׁ:
וְעַתָּה הִנֵּה הֵבֵאתִי אֶת רֵאשִׁית פְּרִי הָאֲדָמָה אֲשֶׁר נָתַתָּה לִּי ה':

And you shall call out and say before the Lord, your God, "An Aramean [sought to] destroy my forefather; he went down to Egypt and sojourned there with a small number of people, and there he became a great, mighty, and numerous nation.

The Egyptians treated us cruelly and afflicted us, and they imposed hard labor upon us.

We cried out to G-d, the G-d of our fathers, and G-d heard our voice and saw our affliction, our toil, and our oppression.

G-d brought us out from Egypt with a strong hand and with an outstretched arm, with great awe, and with miraculous signs and wonders.

He brought us to this place, and He gave us this land, a land flowing with milk and honey.

Now, behold, I have brought the first of the fruit of the ground that you, G-d, have given to me."

TEXT 2

Ibid., v. 11

וְשָׂמַחְתָּ בְכָל הַטּוֹב אֲשֶׁר נָתַן לְךָ ה' אֱלֹקֶיךָ וּלְבֵיתֶךָ

And you shall rejoice in all the good that G-d your G-d has given you and your family.

Roots of Unhappiness

Getting Used to Good

TEXT 3A

Rabbi Bachya ibn Pakuda, Chovot Halevavot,
Introduction to Sha'ar Habechinah

ומשלם בזה לתינוק, שמצאו איש אחד מאנשי החסד במדבר, וחמל
עליו, ויאספהו אל ביתו, ויגדלהו, ויאכילהו, וילבישהו, ויתנדב עליו
בכל הטוב לו, עד שהשכיל והבין אופני דרכי טובתו.
ואחר כן שמע האיש ההוא על אסיר שנפל ביד שונאו, והגיעהו אל
תכלית הצער, והרעב, והעירום ימים רבים, ונכמרו רחמיו על צערו,
ופייס לשונאו, עד שהתירו ומחל לו את דמיו, ויאספהו האיש אל
ביתו, והיטיב לו במקצת הטוב אשר היטיב בו לתינוק.

Rabbi Bachya ibn Pakuda
11th century
Moral philosopher and author. Ibn Pakuda lived in Muslim Spain, but little else is known about his life. *Chovot Halevavot* (*Duties of the Heart*), his major work, was intended to be a guide for attaining spiritual perfection. Originally written in Judeo-Arabic and published in 1080, it was later translated into Hebrew and published in 1161 by Judah ibn Tibbon, a scion of the famous family of translators. Ibn Pakuda had a strong influence on Jewish pietistic literature.

A parable:

There was once an infant found in the desert by a kindhearted individual. The benevolent man took pity on the child, carried him to his home, brought him up, fed him, clothed him, and provided him generously with all that was good, until the child was old enough to understand and comprehend the many benefits he had received.

The same benefactor heard of a man who had fallen into the hands of his enemy and had, for a long time, been treated with extreme cruelty, starved, and kept naked. The benevolent man's compassion was aroused. He appeased the enemy and convinced him to free the prisoner and forgive his debt, and he brought the man to his home. The kindness that he showed this man was a fraction of the kindness he showed the child.

TEXT 3B

Ibid.

> והיה האסיר מכיר בטובת האיש עליו ומודה עליה, יותר מן התינוק שגדל בה, מפני שיצא מעניין העוני והצער אל עניין הטובה והשלווה בעת שהכרתו בה גמורה...והתינוק לא הבין מעלת הטובה עליו, אף על פי שהתחזקה הכרתו והתיישב בדעתו, מפני שהיה רגיל בה מימי נערותו.

The freed prisoner appreciated the man's kindness and thanked him more than the child who grew up with such kindness. For he had left a state of poverty and pain for a state of goodness and tranquility when he was fully mature… But the child did not comprehend the magnitude of his benefactor's kindness, even when he grew older and matured, for he was accustomed to this kindness from his childhood.

The More the Merrier?

TEXT 4

Midrash Kohelet Rabah, 1:13

אין אדם יוצא מן העולם וחצי תאוותו בידו.
אלא אן אית ליה מאה, בעי למעבד יתהון תרתין מאוון. ואן אית
ליה תרתי מאוון, בעי למעבד יתהון ארבעה מאה.

No person leaves this world with even half of his desires fulfilled.

When we have one hundred, we want to make of it two hundred; when we have two hundred, we want to make of it four hundred.

Kohelet Rabah

A Midrashic text on the Book of Ecclesiastes. *Midrash* is the designation of a particular genre of rabbinic literature. The term Midrash is derived from the root *d-r-sh (dalet-raish-shin)*, which means "to search," "to examine," and "to investigate." This particular Midrash provides textual exegeses and develops and illustrates moral principles. It was first printed in Pesaro, Italy, in 1519, together with four other Midrashic works on the other four biblical *megilot*.

Looking the Wrong Way

TEXT 5

Rabbi Bachya ibn Pakuda, Chovot Halevavot,
Introduction to Sha'ar Habechinah

ויתעלמו מהביט אל טובת הבורא עליהם, מפני שלבם תלוי בעוצם
מה שהם מקוים ממלאות תאוותם והשלמת משאלותם. כי כל
אשר יגיעו ממנו אל מעלה, מבקשים מה שהוא למעלה ממנו,
ודורשים מה שאחריה.

People neglect to contemplate the benefits G-d bestows
upon them because the sole aspiration on which their
hearts are fixed is further satisfaction of their desires
and fulfillment of their wishes. Whatever stage of suc-
cess they attain, they seek to proceed higher and further.

More About More

TEXT 6

Rabbi Yosef Yitzchak Schneersohn of Lubavitch,
Sefer Hama'amarim 5710, pp. 239–240

דלבד זאת מה שבטבע האדם מתולדתו הוא דמי שיש לו מנה
רוצה מאתים, ומשום זה אין אדם מת וחצי תאוותו בידו, אשר כן
הוא גם במי שאינו מורגש, הנה מלבד זאת הנה המורגש, שחושב
שמגיע לו הרבה ויוצא מגדר מהותו העצמי, על כן הנה שמחתו מה
ששמח בהטוב שיש לו הנה לא זו שאינה שמחה שלימה, אלא עוד
גורם עצבות משום העדר ההסתפקות. דמצד מעלת מהותו הוא
תמיד עצב, כי הכל, הן מה שנותנים לו מן השמים בבני חיי ומזונא,
והן הכבוד שחולקין לו בני אדם, אינו כלל כפי המגיע לו לפי מהותו
הנעלה בעיני עצמו.

Rabbi Yosef Yitzchak Schneersohn
(Rayatz, Frierdiker Rebbe, Previous Rebbe)
1880–1950

Chasidic rebbe, prolific writer, and Jewish activist. Rabbi Yosef Yitzchak, the 6th leader of the Chabad movement, actively promoted Jewish religious practice in Soviet Russia and was arrested for these activities. After his release from prison and exile, he settled in Warsaw, Poland, from where he fled Nazi occupation, and arrived in New York in 1940. Settling in Brooklyn, Rabbi Schneersohn worked to revitalize American Jewish life. His son-in law, Rabbi Menachem Mendel Schneerson, succeeded him as the leader of the Chabad movement.

By nature, "a person who has one hundred desires two hundred" and therefore, "no person leaves this world with even half of his desires fulfilled." This applies even more so to one who is self-absorbed. He loses sight of who he really is and thinks he deserves more. Due to his perpetual dissatisfaction, not only is his happiness with what he has incomplete, he is actually distressed by it. He overinflates his importance and is therefore always distressed, inasmuch as all that he is given by G-d—family, health, and sustenance—and the honor he is accorded by others, is not adequate for his esteemed nature, as he perceives it.

Overcoming the Hedonic Treadmill

Adopting the Right Attitude

TEXT 7

Bereishit (Genesis) 33:9–11

וַיֹּאמֶר עֵשָׂו יֶשׁ לִי רָב אָחִי יְהִי לְךָ אֲשֶׁר לָךְ:
וַיֹּאמֶר יַעֲקֹב אַל נָא אִם נָא מָצָאתִי חֵן בְּעֵינֶיךָ וְלָקַחְתָּ מִנְחָתִי מִיָּדִי כִּי
עַל כֵּן רָאִיתִי פָנֶיךָ כִּרְאֹת פְּנֵי אֱלֹקִים וַתִּרְצֵנִי:
קַח נָא אֶת בִּרְכָתִי אֲשֶׁר הֻבָאת לָךְ כִּי חַנַּנִי אֱלֹקִים וְכִי יֶשׁ לִי כֹל וַיִּפְצַר
בּוֹ וַיִּקָּח:

Esau said, "I have plenty, my brother; let what you have remain yours."

Thereupon Jacob said, "Please no! If indeed I have found favor in your eyes, then you shall take my gift from my hand, because I have seen your face, which is like seeing the face of an angel, and you have accepted me.

"Now, take my gift, which has been brought to you, for G-d has favored me, and I have everything." He prevailed upon him, and he took it.

Habitude of Gratitude

TEXT 8

Rabbi Shalom Dovber Schneersohn, Sefer Hama'amarim 5659, p. 5

כשמדבר דברי אהבה, שהדיבור מקבל אז ממדת אהבה שבנפשו,
הנה אנו רואין שהדיבור מוסיף אור בהאהבה, שעל ידי שמדבר בה
מאיר בו האור האהבה ביותר ומתפעל ביותר בנפשו באהבה וחיבה
להדבר ההוא . . .
וכן הוא בכל המדות: כשאינם באים בדיבור, יתקטן ויתמעט
התפעלות המדות עד שמתעלמים לגמרי. ולהיפך על ידי שבאים
בדיבור, מתרבים ומתרחבים ביותר.

Rabbi Shalom Dovber Schneersohn (Rashab)
1860– 1920
Chasidic rebbe. Rabbi Shalom Dovber became the fifth leader of the Chabad movement upon the passing of his father, Rabbi Shmuel of Lubavitch. He established the Lubavitch network of *yeshivot* called Tomchei Temimim. He authored many volumes of chasidic discourses and is renowned for his lucid and thorough explanations of kabbalistic concepts.

When a person pours his feelings of love into words, the act of speaking these words fuels and intensifies the love. Through speaking about it, the emotional energy radiates with more passion, and the person is aroused with more love and fondness for the object of his or her love. . . .

The same applies to all emotions: when they are not expressed through speech, they are reduced until they completely dissipate. When they are expressed verbally, they augment and grow considerably.

Two Separate Mitzvot

TEXT 9

Rabbi Aharon Halevi of Barcelona, Sefer HaChinuch, Mitzvah 606

**Rabbi Aharon Halevi
of Barcelona**
(Re'ah)
1235–1290

Born in Gerona, Spain. Rabbi,
talmudist, and authority on
Jewish law. Rabbi Aharon
studied under Nachmanides
and under his father,
Rabbi Yosef Halevi, and
corresponded with the leading
talmudic scholars of his
generation. His explanations
on the Rashba's halachic
code, *Torat Habayit*, entitled
Bedek Habayit, are integral
in the formation of Jewish
law. Rabbi Aharon was
considered by some to be the
anonymous author of *Sefer
Hachinuch*, a compendium
of the 613 commandments.

מצות קריאה על הבכורים. שנצטוינו בהביאנו הבכורים למקדש
לקרות עליהם הכתובים אלו הנזכרים בפרשה זו, והן, מארמי אבד
אבי עד הנה הבאתי את ראשית פרי האדמה אשר נתתה לי ה׳.
ועל זה נאמר וענית ואמרת לפני ה׳ אלקיך וגו׳. וזאת המצוה יקראו
זכרונם לברכה מקרא בכורים.

The commandment to proclaim over bikurim: *We
were commanded that upon bringing* bikurim *to the
Temple, we must read over them the verses written in
this passage, from "An Aramean sought to destroy my
forefather" until "Now, behold, I have brought the first
of the fruit of the ground that you, G-d, have given to
me"… This mitzvah is called* mikrah bikurim.

Thanks in Prayer

TEXT 10

Midrash Tanchuma, Parashat Ki Tavo 1

צפה משה ברוח הקודש וראה שבית המקדש עתיד ליחרב
והבכורים עתידין ליפסק, עמד והתקין לישראל שיהיו מתפללין
שלשה פעמים בכל יום.

*Moses foresaw that the Temple would be destroyed
and the offering of the first fruits would cease. He took
initiative and ordained that the Jewish people should
pray three times a day.*

Midrash Tanchuma
A midrashic work bearing the
name of Rabbi Tanchuma, a
4th century Talmudic sage
quoted often in this work.
Midrash is the designation of
a particular genre of rabbinic
literature usually forming
a running commentary on
specific books of the Bible.
Midrash Tanchuma provides
textual exegeses, expounds
upon the biblical narrative,
and develops and illustrates
moral principles. *Tanchuma*
is unique in that many of its
sections commence with a
halachic discussion, which
subsequently leads into
non-halachic teachings.

TEXT 11A

Siddur, Prayer upon Rising

מוֹדֶה אֲנִי לְפָנֶיךָ מֶלֶךְ חַי וְקַיָּם, שֶׁהֶחֱזַרְתָּ בִּי נִשְׁמָתִי בְּחֶמְלָה.
רַבָּה אֱמוּנָתֶךָ.

*I thank you, living and eternal King, for mercifully
restoring my soul within me. Your faithfulness is great.*

Sidur Tehilat Hashem
One of the prayer books
that follow the tradition of
the Arizal, as established
by Rabbi Shneur Zalman of
Liadi. It was first published
in New York in 1945.

TEXT 11B

Siddur, Morning Blessings

בָּרוּךְ אַתָּה ה' אֱלֹקֵינוּ מֶלֶךְ הָעוֹלָם, אֲשֶׁר יָצַר אֶת הָאָדָם בְּחָכְמָה.
וּבָרָא בוֹ נְקָבִים נְקָבִים. חֲלוּלִים חֲלוּלִים. גָּלוּי וְיָדוּעַ לִפְנֵי כִסֵּא כְבוֹדֶךָ
שֶׁאִם יִסָּתֵם אֶחָד מֵהֶם, אוֹ אִם יִפָּתַח אֶחָד מֵהֶם, אִי אֶפְשָׁר לְהִתְקַיֵּם
אֲפִלּוּ שָׁעָה אֶחָת. בָּרוּךְ אַתָּה ה', רוֹפֵא כָל בָּשָׂר וּמַפְלִיא לַעֲשׂוֹת.

*Blessed are You, Lord our G-d, Sovereign of the uni-
verse, who formed man with wisdom, and created
within him many orifices and cavities. It is revealed
and known before the throne of Your glory that if but
one were to be blocked, or one of them were to rup-
ture, it would be impossible to survive even for a short
while. Blessed are You, G-d, Who heals all flesh and
performs wonders.*

TEXT 11C

Siddur, Eighteenth blessing of the Amidah

מוֹדִים אֲנַחְנוּ לָךְ שָׁאַתָּה הוּא ה' אֱלֹקֵינוּ וֵאלֹקֵי אֲבוֹתֵינוּ לְעוֹלָם וָעֶד.
צוּר חַיֵּינוּ, מָגֵן יִשְׁעֵנוּ, אַתָּה הוּא לְדוֹר וָדוֹר. נוֹדֶה לְךָ וּנְסַפֵּר תְּהִלָּתֶךָ
עַל חַיֵּינוּ הַמְּסוּרִים בְּיָדֶךָ, וְעַל נִשְׁמוֹתֵינוּ הַפְּקוּדוֹת לָךְ, וְעַל נִסֶּיךָ שֶׁבְּכָל
יוֹם עִמָּנוּ, וְעַל נִפְלְאוֹתֶיךָ וְטוֹבוֹתֶיךָ שֶׁבְּכָל עֵת, עֶרֶב וָבֹקֶר וְצָהֳרָיִם...

We thankfully acknowledge that You are the Lord our G-d and the G-d of our ancestors, forever. You are the rock of our lives, the shield of our salvation in every generation. We shall thank You and recount Your praise, evening, morning, and noon, for our lives that are in Your hand, for our souls that are entrusted to You, for Your miracles that are with us daily, and for Your continuous wonders and goodness.

The Real Reason to Be Grateful

Appreciating the Giver

TEXT 12

Chinuch, Ibid.

משרשי המצוה. לפי שהאדם מעורר מחשבותיו ומציר בלבבו
האמת בכח דברי פיו, על כן, בהיטיב אליו השם ברוך הוא ובברכו
אותו ואת אדמתו לעשות פרות וזכה להביאם לבית אלהינו ראוי לו
לעורר לבו בדברי פיהו ולחשב כי הכל הגיע אליו מאת אדון העולם,
ויספר חסדיו יתברך עלינו ועל כל עם ישראל דרך כלל.
ועל כן, מתחיל בענין יעקב אבינו שחלצו ה' מיד לבן, וענין עבודת
המצריים בנו, והצילנו הוא ברוך הוא מידם, ואחר השבח מבקש
מלפניו להתמיד הברכה עליו, ומתוך התעוררות נפשו בשבח השם
ובטובו זוכה ומתברכת אותו (נ"א אישו), ועל כן צונו ברוך הוא על
זה, כי חפץ חסד הוא.

When G-d treats [a person] kindly and blesses him
and his land with fruit, thus giving him the privilege
of bringing them to the Temple, he ought to awaken in
his heart and express verbally that everything is from
G-d. He should speak of G-d's kindness upon us and on
all Israel in general.

Therefore, he begins with the story of Jacob our father whom G-d saved from the hands of Laban, and

continues with the story of G-d saving us from our Egyptian oppressors, and asks G-d to constantly bestow His blessing. By awakening in himself expression of G-d's praise and goodness, he further merits G-d's blessing. Therefore, G-d gave us this commandment, for He desires kindness.

True Wealth

TEXT 13

Mishna Avot 4:1

בֶּן זוֹמָא אוֹמֵר:

אֵיזֶהוּ חָכָם? הַלּוֹמֵד מִכָּל אָדָם, שֶׁנֶּאֱמַר: מִכָּל מְלַמְּדַי הִשְׂכַּלְתִּי כִּי עֵדְוֹתֶיךָ שִׂיחָה לִי.

אֵיזֶהוּ גִבּוֹר? הַכּוֹבֵשׁ אֶת יִצְרוֹ, שֶׁנֶּאֱמַר: טוֹב אֶרֶךְ אַפַּיִם מִגִּבּוֹר וּמֹשֵׁל בְּרוּחוֹ מִלֹּכֵד עִיר.

אֵיזֶהוּ עָשִׁיר? הַשָּׂמֵחַ בְּחֶלְקוֹ, שֶׁנֶּאֱמַר: יְגִיעַ כַּפֶּיךָ כִּי תֹאכֵל אַשְׁרֶיךָ וְטוֹב לָךְ. אַשְׁרֶיךָ בָּעוֹלָם הַזֶּה. וְטוֹב לָךְ לָעוֹלָם הַבָּא.

אֵיזֶהוּ מְכֻבָּד? הַמְכַבֵּד אֶת הַבְּרִיּוֹת, שֶׁנֶּאֱמַר: כִּי מְכַבְּדַי אֲכַבֵּד וּבֹזַי יֵקָלּוּ.

Mishnah
The first authoritative work of Jewish law that was codified in writing. The Mishnah contains the oral traditions that were passed down from teacher to student; it supplements, clarifies, and systematizes the commandments of the Torah. Due to the continual persecution of the Jewish people, it became increasingly difficult to guarantee that these traditions would not be forgotten. Rabbi Yehudah Hanasi therefore redacted the Mishnah at the end of the 2nd century. It serves as the foundation for the Talmud.

Ben Zoma would say: Who is wise? One who learns from every man. As is stated, "From all my teachers I have grown wise, for Your testimonials are my meditation."

Who is strong? One who overpowers his inclinations. As is stated, "Better one who is slow to anger than one with might, one who rules his spirit than the captor of a city."

Who is rich? One who is satisfied with his lot. As is stated, "If you eat of the toil of your hands, fortunate are you, and good is to you"; "fortunate are you" in this world, "and good is to you" in the World to Come.

Who is honorable? One who honors his fellows. As is stated, "For those who honor me, I accord honor; those who scorn me shall be demeaned."

TEXT 14

Yirmiyahu (Jeremiah) 9:22

כֹּה אָמַר ה' אַל יִתְהַלֵּל חָכָם בְּחָכְמָתוֹ וְאַל יִתְהַלֵּל הַגִּבּוֹר בִּגְבוּרָתוֹ אַל יִתְהַלֵּל עָשִׁיר בְּעָשְׁרוֹ:
כִּי אִם בְּזֹאת יִתְהַלֵּל הַמִּתְהַלֵּל הַשְׂכֵּל וְיָדֹעַ אוֹתִי כִּי אֲנִי יְהוָה עֹשֶׂה חֶסֶד מִשְׁפָּט וּצְדָקָה בָּאָרֶץ כִּי בְאֵלֶּה חָפַצְתִּי נְאֻם ה':

Thus says G-d: Let not the wise man boast of his wisdom, nor the strong man boast of his strength, nor the rich man boast of his riches.

But let him that boasts exult in this, that he understands and knows Me, for I am G-d Who practices kindness, justice, and righteousness on the earth; for in these things I delight, says G-d.

TEXT 15

Rabbi Yom Tov Lippman Heller, Ikar Tosafot Yom Tov, Avot 4:1

יש להקשות ממה שאמר ירמיה אל יתהלל חכם בחכמתו ואל יתהלל גבור בגבורתו ואל יתהלל עשיר בעשרו כי אם בזאת יתהלל המתהלל השכל וידוע אותי. ונראה לי דלא קשיא, דס״ל לתנא דידן שזה שאמר כי אם השכל וידוע אותי, הוא עצמו בכלל החכמה והגבורה והעושר שזכר. וכך הוא אומר אל יתהלל חכם בחכמתו כי אם שהיא החכמה השכל וידוע אותי. וכן לענין הגבורה והעושר, ולזה שאל התנא איזהו חכם כו׳ שאליו כיון הנביא.

Rabbi YomTov Lippman Heller
1579–1654
Authority on Jewish law; author; flourished in Poland and Germany; often called the "Tosafot YomTov" after the title of this most famous work on the Mishnah. In his youth, he was a student of the Maharal of Prague. In addition to his profound mastery of the Talmud and post-Talmudic commentaries, he was engaged in the study of Kabbalah, philosophy, and grammar, and had a broad grasp of mathematics, astronomy, and natural science. At 18, he was appointed rabbinic judge in Prague, and served there for almost 28 years. Later, he served as rabbi in Nikolsburg, Vienna, Lublin, Brisk, Ludmir, and other communities.

The question arises: Did Yirmiyahu not say, "Let not the wise man boast of his wisdom, nor the strong man boast of his strength, nor the rich man boast of his riches. But let him that boasts exult in this, that he understands and knows Me"? The answer is as follows: Ben Zoma understands that the wisdom, strength, and riches that he mentions are expressions of "that he understands and knows me." The verse is saying, "Let not the wise man boast of his wisdom"—unless that wisdom is part of "understanding and knowing Me." And the same is true of strength and riches.

9

NITZAVIM-VAYELECH

A Call For Unity

Hakhel, *Then and Now*

*Dedicated in honor of the birthday of our friend **Rabbi Bentzion Milecki**, 19 Elul.
May he and his family merit to witness the fulfillment of continuous blessings for
health, happiness, nachas and success in all their endeavors.*

PARASHAH OVERVIEW
Nitzavim-Vayelech

The Parshah of Nitzavim includes some of the most fundamental principles of the Jewish faith:

The unity of Israel: *"You stand today, all of you, before the L-rd your G-d: your* heads, *your* tribes, *your* elders, *your* officers, *and* every Israelite man; your young ones, *your* wives, *the* stranger *in your gate; from your* wood-hewer *to your* water-drawer."

The future redemption: *Moses warns of the exile and desolation of the Land that will result if Israel abandons G-d's laws, but then he prophesies that in the end, "You will return to the L-rd your G-d . . . If your outcasts shall be at the ends of the heavens, from there will the L-rd your G-d gather you . . . and bring you into the Land which your fathers have possessed."*

The practicality of Torah: *"For the mitzvah which I command you this day, it is not beyond you, nor is it remote from you. It is* not in heaven . . . *It is not across the sea . . . Rather, it is* very close *to you, in your* mouth, *in your* heart, *that you may* do it."

Freedom of choice: *"I have set before you life and goodness, and death and evil: in that I command you this day to love G-d, to walk in His ways and to keep His commandments . . . Life and death I have set before you, blessing and curse. And you shall choose life."*

The Parshah of Vayelech ("and he went") recounts the events of Moses' last day of earthly life. "I am one hundred and twenty years old today," he says to the people, "and I can no longer go forth and come in." He transfers the leadership to Joshua, and writes (or concludes writing) the Torah in a scroll which he entrusts to the Levites for safekeeping in the Ark of the Covenant.

The mitzvah of Hakhel ("gather") is given: every seven years, during the festival of Sukkot of the first year of the shemittah cycle, the entire people of Israel—men, women and children—should gather at the Holy Temple in Jerusalem, where the king should read to them from the Torah.

Vayelech concludes with the prediction that the people of Israel will turn away from their covenant with G-d, causing Him to hide His face from them, but also with the promise that the words of the Torah "shall not be forgotten out of the mouths of their descendants."

Lesson 9 / A Call For Unity   167

The Epic Gathering

Hakhel—What is it?

TEXT 1

Devarim (Deuteronomy) 31:10-12

וַיְצַו מֹשֶׁה אוֹתָם לֵאמֹר מִקֵּץ שֶׁבַע שָׁנִים בְּמֹעֵד שְׁנַת הַשְּׁמִטָּה
בְּחַג הַסֻּכּוֹת:
בְּבוֹא כָל יִשְׂרָאֵל לֵרָאוֹת אֶת פְּנֵי ה' אֱלֹקֶיךָ בַּמָּקוֹם אֲשֶׁר יִבְחָר תִּקְרָא
אֶת הַתּוֹרָה הַזֹּאת נֶגֶד כָּל יִשְׂרָאֵל בְּאָזְנֵיהֶם:
הַקְהֵל אֶת הָעָם הָאֲנָשִׁים וְהַנָּשִׁים וְהַטַּף וְגֵרְךָ אֲשֶׁר בִּשְׁעָרֶיךָ לְמַעַן
יִשְׁמְעוּ וּלְמַעַן יִלְמְדוּ וְיָרְאוּ אֶת ה' אֱלֹקֵיכֶם וְשָׁמְרוּ לַעֲשׂוֹת אֶת כָּל
דִּבְרֵי הַתּוֹרָה הַזֹּאת:

Then, Moses commanded them, saying, "At the end of [every] seven years, at an appointed time, in the Festival of Succoth, [after] the year of release,

When all Israel comes to appear before the Lord, your G-d, in the place He will choose, you shall read this Torah before all Israel, in their ears.

Assemble the people: the men, the women, and the children, and your stranger in your cities, in order that they hear, and in order that they learn and fear the Lord, your G-d, and they will observe to do all the words of this Torah.

When

TEXT 2

Talmud Tractate Sotah, 41:1

וכל הני למה לי? צריכי — דאי כתב רחמנא "מקץ", הוה אמינא נימנו
מהשתא ואף על גב דלא מתרמי בשמיטה, כתב רחמנא "שמיטה".
ואי כתב רחמנא "שמיטה", הוה אמינא בסוף שמיטה, כתב רחמנא
"במועד". ואי כתב "במועד" הוה אמינא מריש שתא, כתב רחמנא
"בחג הסוכות".

ואי כתב רחמנא "בחג הסוכות" הוה אמינא אפילו יום טוב אחרון,
כתב רחמנא "בבוא כל ישראל", מאתחלתא דמועד.

Babylonian Talmud
A literary work of monumental proportions that draws upon the legal, spiritual, intellectual, ethical, and historical traditions of Judaism. The 37 tractates of the Babylonian Talmud contain the teachings of the Jewish sages from the period after the destruction of the 2nd Temple through the 5th century CE. It has served as the primary vehicle for the transmission of the Oral Law and the education of Jews over the centuries; it is the entry point for all subsequent legal, ethical, and theological Jewish scholarship.

Why are all these verses necessary? For if the Torah only stated "at the end of seven years," it might be understood that the count starts from the time of the command, even if it weren't the shemitah *year. So, the verse specified* shemitah.

And if the verse specified that this takes place after the shemitah *year, we might think it refers to the end of the* shemitah *year. So, the verse states, "At an appointed time." And if the verse wrote only "at an appointed time," we might think it refers to the beginning of the year. So, the verse states, "In the festival of Sukkot."*

And if the verse stated "in the festival of Sukkot," we might think it refers to the last day of the holiday. So, the verse states, "When all Israel comes to appear," i.e., at the beginning of the holiday.

Where?

TEXT 3

Maimonides, Mishneh Torah, Hilchot Chagigah 3:1-3

**Rabbi Moshe
ben Maimon**
(Maimonides, Rambam)
1135–1204
Halachist, philosopher, author,
and physician. Maimonides
was born in Cordoba, Spain.
After the conquest of Cordoba
by the Almohads, he fled
Spain and eventually settled
in Cairo, Egypt. There, he
became the leader of the
Jewish community and served
as court physician to the vizier
of Egypt. He is most noted
for authoring the *Mishneh
Torah*, an encyclopedic
arrangement of Jewish law,
and for his philosophical
work, *Guide for the Perplexed*.
His rulings on Jewish law
are integral to the formation
of halachic consensus.

מצות עשה להקהיל כל ישראל אנשים ונשים וטף בכל מוצאי שמיטה בעלותם לרגל ולקרות באזניהם מן התורה . . ובעזרת הנשים היו קורין.

It is a positive commandment to gather together the entire Jewish people —men, women, and children—after every Sabbatical year when they ascend for the pilgrimage holiday and to read so that they hear passages from the Torah… The reading was held in the Women's Courtyard.

Who?

TEXT 4

Devarim, loc. cit. v. 13

וּבְנֵיהֶם אֲשֶׁר לֹא יָדְעוּ יִשְׁמְעוּ וְלָמְדוּ לְיִרְאָה אֶת יְהֹוָה אֱלֹהֵיכֶם כָּל
הַיָּמִים אֲשֶׁר אַתֶּם חַיִּים עַל הָאֲדָמָה אֲשֶׁר אַתֶּם עֹבְרִים אֶת הַיַּרְדֵּן
שָׁמָּה לְרִשְׁתָּהּ:

*And their children, who did not know, will hear and
learn to fear the Lord, your G-d, all the days that you
live on the land, to which you are crossing the Jordan,
to possess.*

TEXT 5

Rabbi Moshe Sofer, Chatam Sofer al HaTorah, Parashat Vayelech

רק אומר לפי הבנה זו דבניהם אשר לא ידעו המה קטני קטנים
מפורש בקרא טעם ביאתם ובניהם אשר לא ידעו ישמעו ולמדו
פירוש על פי מה שכתוב הירושלמי אמו של רבי יהושע בן חנניה
הכניסה עריסה שלו בבית המדרש כדי שיכנס באזנו קול דברי
תורה וזה מסוגל לכשיגדל שיהיה תלמיד חכם וצדיק.
והכי נמי אחר שציוה להביא הטף שהגיעו לחינוך שוב אמר ובניהם
אשר לא ידעו שלח הגיעו לחינוך מכל מקום ישמעו ויכנם באזניהם
קול המולה של תורה וילמדו בעתיד אחר זמן לכשיגדל.

Rabbi Moshe Sofer
(*Chatam Sofer*)
1762–1839
A leading rabbinical authority
of the 19th century. Born
in Frankfurt am Main,
Chatam Sofer ultimately
accepted the rabbinate of
Pressburg (now Bratislava),
Slovakia. Serving as rabbi
and head of the yeshivah
that he established, Rabbi
Sofer maintained a strong
traditionalist perspective,
opposing deviation from
Jewish tradition. *Chatam Sofer*
is the title of his collection
of halachic responsa and his
commentary to the Talmud.

"Their children who did not know" refers to tiny infants. Yet we can understand how they will "hear and learn," as the Jerusalem Talmud states, "Rabbi Yochanan ben Zakai's mother brought his cradle into the study hall, so that the sound of Torah study would enter his ears. This would prepare him to become a Torah scholar and a tzadik when he grew older."

Likewise, after the verse commands us to bring older children [to the hakhel *gathering], it then says to bring the "children who did not know," for though they are not yet old enough to understand, the words of Torah will nevertheless enter their ears, and this will prepare them to learn in the future, when they grow older.*

Faith and Fanfare

Verses that Inspire

TEXT 6A

Mishneh Torah, Ibid. 3:1

> מצות עשה להקהיל כל ישראל אנשים ונשים וטף . . ולקרות
> באזניהם מן התורה פרשיות שהן מזרזות אותן במצות ומחזקות
> ידיהם בדת האמת.

*It is a positive commandment to gather together the
entire Jewish people—men, women, and children…
and to read so that they hear passages from the Torah
that encourage them to perform* mitzvot *and strengthen
them in the true faith.*

TEXT 6B

Mishneh Torah, Ibid. 3:3

> מהיכן הוא קורא? מתחילת חומש אלה הדברים עד סוף פרשת
> שמע, ומדלג ל'והיה אם שמוע וגו'' ומדלג ל'עשר תעשר' וקורא
> מ'עשר תעשר' על הסדר עד סוף ברכות וקללות עד 'מלבד הברית
> אשר כרת אתם בחורב' ופוסק.

From which passages in the Torah should he read? He starts from the beginning of Deuteronomy until the end of the passage Shema. He then skips to the passage vehayah im shamoa, and then skips to the passage asair te'asair. He then reads from that passage until the end of the blessing and curses, i.e., until the phrase, "Besides the covenant He established with them in Choreb" where he concludes.

TEXT 7

Rashi, Sotah 41a

Rabbi Shlomo Yitzchaki
(Rashi)
1040–1105

Most noted biblical and Talmudic commentator. Born in Troyes, France, Rashi studied in the famed *yeshivot* of Mainz and Worms. His commentaries on the Pentateuch and the Talmud, which focus on the straightforward meaning of the text, appear in virtually every edition of the Talmud and Bible.

וקורא . . 'שמע' קבלת מלכות שמים, 'והיה אם שמוע' קבלת עול מצות . . וכן ברכות וקללות קבלת בריתות של תורה, ומשמיע לרבים 'עשר תעשר' 'כי תכלה לעשר' מפני שהוא זמן אסיף ומתנות עניים והפרשת תרומות ומעשרות.

He reads... "Shema" which expresses acceptance of G-d's Kingship, and "vehaya im shamoa" which expresses acceptance of the commandments... He also reads the verses containing the blessings and curses, which express acceptance of the Torah's covenants, and he reads "asair te'asair" and "ki tichale le'asair," for it is the time of gathering produce, when produce is distributed to the poor, and terumah and ma'aser are set aside.

Due Pomp and Ceremony

TEXT 8

Mishneh Torah, ad loc 3:4

כיצד הוא קורא? תוקעין בחצוצרות בכל ירושלים כדי להקהיל את
העם ומביאין בימה גדולה ושל עץ היתה ומעמידין אותה באמצע
עזרת נשים והמלך עולה ויושב עליה כדי שישמעו קריאתו וכל
ישראל העולים לחג מתקבצין סביביו וחזן הכנסת נוטל ספר תורה
ונותנו לראש הכנסת וראש הכנסת נותנו לסגן וסגן לכהן גדול וכהן
גדול למלך כדי להדרו ברוב בני אדם והמלך מקבלו כשהוא עומד
ואם רצה ישב ופותח ורואה ומברך כדרך שמברך כל קורא בתורה
בבית הכנסת וקורא הפרשיות שאמרנו עד שהוא גומר וגולל ומברך
לאחריה כדרך שמברכין בבתי כנסיות.

How is the reading conducted? Trumpets are sounded throughout Jerusalem to gather the people. A large wooden platform is brought and set up in the center of the Women's Courtyard. The King ascends and sits on it so that the people will be able to hear his reading. All of the Jewish people who made the festive pilgrimage gather around him. The attendant of the synagogue would take the Torah scroll and give it to the head of the synagogue. He would give it to the deputy, who would give it to the High Priest, who would give it to the King. The transfer involved many people as an expression of respect. The King accepted the scroll while standing. If he desired, he could sit when reading. He opened it, looked at it, and recited the blessings like anyone who is reading the Torah in a synagogue.

No Microphone?

TEXT 9

Rabbi Yehuda Leib Alter of Gur, Sefat Emet al Hatorah, Vayelech 5642

Rabbi Yehudah Aryeh Leib Alter
(Sefat Emet)
1847–1905 Chasidic master and scholar. Rabbi Yehudah Aryeh Leib Alter assumed the leadership of the Chasidic dynasty of Gur (Gora), a town near Warsaw, Poland, at the age of 23. He was the grandson and successor of Rabbi Yitzchak Meir of Gur, the founder of the Gur dynasty. He is commonly referred to as the *Sefat Emet*, after the title of his commentaries on the Torah and Talmud.

כי בוודאי היה סיוע משמים להמלך כי מצד הטבע אין באפשרות להשמיע באזני כל קהל ישראל.

Certainly, the King received Heavenly assistance, for it is physically impossible for his voice to have been heard by the entire congregation of Jewish people.

(Just Like) Hakhel

TEXT 10

Nechemia (Nehemiah) 1:1-8

וַיֵּאָסְפוּ כָל הָעָם כְּאִישׁ אֶחָד אֶל הָרְחוֹב אֲשֶׁר לִפְנֵי שַׁעַר הַמָּיִם
וַיֹּאמְרוּ לְעֶזְרָא הַסֹּפֵר לְהָבִיא אֶת סֵפֶר תּוֹרַת מֹשֶׁה אֲשֶׁר צִוָּה ה'
אֶת יִשְׂרָאֵל:
וַיָּבִיא עֶזְרָא הַכֹּהֵן אֶת הַתּוֹרָה לִפְנֵי הַקָּהָל מֵאִישׁ וְעַד אִשָּׁה וְכֹל מֵבִין
לִשְׁמֹעַ בְּיוֹם אֶחָד לַחֹדֶשׁ הַשְּׁבִיעִי:
וַיִּקְרָא בוֹ לִפְנֵי הָרְחוֹב אֲשֶׁר לִפְנֵי שַׁעַר הַמַּיִם מִן הָאוֹר עַד מַחֲצִית
הַיּוֹם נֶגֶד הָאֲנָשִׁים וְהַנָּשִׁים וְהַמְּבִינִים וְאָזְנֵי כָל הָעָם אֶל סֵפֶר הַתּוֹרָה:
וַיַּעֲמֹד עֶזְרָא הַסֹּפֵר עַל מִגְדַּל עֵץ אֲשֶׁר עָשׂוּ לַדָּבָר וַיַּעֲמֹד אֶצְלוֹ
מַתִּתְיָה וְשֶׁמַע וַעֲנָיָה וְאוּרִיָּה וְחִלְקִיָּה וּמַעֲשֵׂיָה עַל יְמִינוֹ וּמִשְּׂמֹאלוֹ
פְּדָיָה וּמִישָׁאֵל וּמַלְכִּיָּה וְחָשֻׁם וְחַשְׁבַּדָּנָה זְכַרְיָה מְשֻׁלָּם:
וַיִּפְתַּח עֶזְרָא הַסֵּפֶר לְעֵינֵי כָל הָעָם כִּי מֵעַל כָּל הָעָם הָיָה וּכְפִתְחוֹ
עָמְדוּ כָל הָעָם:
וַיְבָרֶךְ עֶזְרָא אֶת ה' הָאֱלֹקִים הַגָּדוֹל וַיַּעֲנוּ כָל הָעָם אָמֵן אָמֵן בְּמֹעַל
יְדֵיהֶם וַיִּקְּדוּ וַיִּשְׁתַּחֲוֻ לַה' אַפַּיִם אָרְצָה:
וְיֵשׁוּעַ וּבָנִי וְשֵׁרֵבְיָה יָמִין עַקּוּב שַׁבְּתַי הוֹדִיָּה מַעֲשֵׂיָה קְלִיטָא עֲזַרְיָה
יוֹזָבָד חָנָן פְּלָאיָה וְהַלְוִיִּם מְבִינִים אֶת הָעָם לַתּוֹרָה וְהָעָם עַל עָמְדָם:
וַיִּקְרְאוּ בַסֵּפֶר בְּתוֹרַת הָאֱלֹקִים מְפֹרָשׁ וְשׂוֹם שֶׂכֶל וַיָּבִינוּ בַּמִּקְרָא.

Now all the people gathered as one man to the square that was before the Water Gate, and they said to Ezra the scholar to bring the scroll of the Law of Moses, which G-d had commanded Israel.

And Ezra the priest brought the Law before the congregation, both men and women, and all who could hear with understanding, on the first day of the seventh month.

And he read in it before the square that was before the Water Gate from the [first] light until midday in the presence of the men and the women and those who understood, and the ears of all the people were [attentive] to the Scroll of the Law.

And Ezra the scholar stood on a wooden tower that they had made for the purpose, and there stood beside him Mattithiah, and Shema, and Anaiah, and Uriah, and Hilkiah, and Maaseiah on his right, and on his left Pedaiah, Mishael, Malkijah, Hashum, Hashbadanah, Zechariah, [and] Meshullam.

And Ezra opened the scroll before the eyes of the entire people, for he was above all the people, and when he opened it, all the people stood.

And Ezra blessed the Lord, the great G-d, and all the people answered, "Amen, Amen," with the uplifting of their hands, and they bent their heads and prostrated themselves to G-d on their faces to the ground.

And Jeshua, and Bani, and Sherebiah, Jamin, Akkub, Shabbethai, Hodiah, Maaseiah, Kelita, Azariah, Jozabad, Hanan, Pelaiah, and the Levites explained the Law to the people, and the people stood in their place.

And they read in the scroll, in the Law of G-d, distinctly, and gave sense, and they explained the reading to them.

Sinai Revisited

A Lasting Impact

TEXT 11

Rabbi Aharon Halevi of Barcelona, Sefer Hachinuch, Mitzvah 612

ולהיות הקול יוצא בתוך כל העם, אנשים ונשים וטף לאמור מה
הקיבוץ הרב הזה שנתקבצנו יחד כלנו?

ותהיה התשובה – לשמוע דברי התורה שהיא כל עיקרנו והודנו
ותפארתנו, ויבואו מתוך כך לספר בגודל שבחה והוד ערכה ויכניסו
הכל בלבם חשקה, ועם החשק בה ילמדו לדעת את ה' ויזכו לטובה,
וישמח ה' במעשיו, וכעניין שכתוב בפירוש בזאת המצוה 'ולמען
ילמדו ויראו את ה''.

Rabbi Aharon Halevi of Barcelona
(Re'ah)
1235–1290
Born in Gerona, Spain. Rabbi, talmudist, and authority on Jewish law. Rabbi Aharon studied under Nachmanides and under his father, Rabbi Yosef Halevi, and corresponded with the leading talmudic scholars of his generation. His explanations on the Rashba's halachic code, *Torat Habayit*, entitled *Bedek Habayit*, are integral in the formation of Jewish law. Rabbi Aharon was considered by some to be the anonymous author of *Sefer Hachinuch*, a compendium of the 613 commandments.

The intent is for the entire congregation to see the gathering, and wonder, "What is this great gathering all about?"

And the answer will be: To hear the words of the Torah, for the Torah is the very basis of our nation, and our pride and glory. The congregation will thereby be moved to speak of and ingrain in their hearts the great praise of the Torah and its exalted quality. With this inspiration, they will learn to know G-d and merit goodness. G-d will thus rejoice in His creation, as the verse states regarding this commandment [of hakhel*], "so that they learn and fear G-d."*

Mini-Sinai

TEXT 12

Maimonides, Mishneh Torah, Hilchot Chagigah, 3:6

וגרים שאינן מכירין חייבין להכין לבם ולהקשיב אזנם לשמוע
באימה ויראה וגילה ברעדה כיום שניתנה בו בסיני אפילו חכמים
גדולים שיודעים כל התורה כולה חייבין לשמוע בכוונה גדולה יתרה.
ומי שאינו יכול לשמוע מכוין לבו לקריאה זו שלא קבעה הכתוב
אלא לחזק דת האמת ויראה עצמו כאילו עתה נצטוה בה ומפי
הגבורה שומעה שהמלך שליח הוא להשמיע דברי הא-ל.

Converts who do not understand are obligated to
concentrate their attention and direct their hearing,
listening with reverence and awe, and rejoicing while
trembling as on the day the Torah was given at Sinai.
Even great Sages who know the entire Torah are obligated to listen with exceedingly great concentration.

One who is unable to hear should focus his attention
on this reading, for Scripture established it solely to
strengthen the true faith. He should see himself as if
he was just now commanded regarding the Torah and
heard it from the Almighty. For the King is an agent to
make known the word of G-d.

The More the Merrier?

TEXT 13A

Rabbi Don Yitzchak Abarbanel, Abarbanel, Parshat Vayelech

למה צוה יתברך שתהיה קריאת התורה מקץ שבע שנים במועד שנת השמטה בחג הסוכות. והיה ראוי שתקרא שנה בשנה וגם בכל רגל ורגל בעלות ישראל לבית הבחירה היה ראוי שתקרא התורה בפניהם. ולמה נתיחד אמרו משבע שנים לשבע שנים.

Why did G-d command to read the Torah at the end of seven years, during Sukkot? Wouldn't it have been more appropriate to read it every single year, and every single holiday, when the Jewish people would ascend to the Temple? So why was it limited to once in seven years?

Rabbi Don Yitzchak Abarbanel
1437–1508
Biblical exegete and statesman. Abarbanel was born in Lisbon, Portugal, and served as a minister in the court of King Alfonso V of Portugal. After intrigues at court led to accusations against him, he fled to Spain, where he once again served as a counselor to royalty. It is claimed that Abarbanel offered King Ferdinand and Queen Isabella large sums of money for the revocation of their Edict of Expulsion of 1492, but to no avail. After the expulsion, he eventually settled in Italy where he wrote a commentary on Scripture, as well as other venerated works.

TEXT 13B

Ibid.

הנה הסבה בזה היתה לפי שהקב"ה השגיח שיהיו דברי תורה חביבים
על ישראל ושמלבד הלימוד הפרטי שיחידי הסגולה הכהנים הלוים
החכמים והשופטים ילמדו את התורה ויהגו בה יומם ולילה. עוד
בפומבי גדול יקרא הגדול שבעם שהוא המלך או השופט את ספר
התורה נגד כל ישראל כדי שישמעו ויתפעלו לבותיהם מהדברים
ומכבוד המדבר והקורא.
ואם היה זה בכל שנה היה הדבר נקל בעיניהם כמאמר שלמה הוקר
רגליך מבית רעך וגו'. ולכן צוה שמהשנים לא תהיה הקריאה תדירה
בכל שנה כי אם בשנת השמיטה.

The reason is that G-d wanted the words of the Torah to be dear to the Jewish people, so that besides for personal Torah study of the Kohanim, the Levites, the Sages and the Judges, who would toil in Torah study day and night, the Torah would also be read in public by the leader of the nation, the King or Judge, before the entire Jewish people. In this manner, they could all hear and be inspired by words and by the honor of the person reading.

Now, if this were to take place every single year, the event would be less momentous in their eyes, as Solomon said, "Visit your neighbor sparingly, [lest he become sated with you and hate you.]" Therefore, G-d commanded that the reading should not be done frequently, but rather only at the outset of the year following the shemitah *year.*

TEXT 14

Rabbi Yisrael Baal Shem Tov, Keter Shem Tov 1:121

כי תענוג תמידי נעשה טבע ואינו תענוג, לכך האדם עולה ויורד בעבודת השם יתברך כדי שיהיה [לו] תענוג שהוא עיקר עבודת השם יתברך.

A constant pleasure ultimately becomes an ordinary part of life, and is thus no longer pleasure. Therefore, a person fluctuates in his or her divine service, so that they will have pleasure, which is essential to divine service.

Rabbi Yisrael Baal Shem Tov (Besht)
1698–1760
Founder of the Chasidic movement. Born in Slutsk, Belarus, the Baal Shem Tov was orphaned as a child. He served as a teacher's assistant and clay digger before founding the Chasidic movement and revolutionizing the Jewish world with his emphasis on prayer, joy, and love for every Jew, regardless of his or her level of Torah knowledge.

The Year of Study and Prayer

TEXT 15

The Lubavitcher Rebbe, Shaarei Hamoadim, Shemini Atzeret-Simchat Torah, p. 374

אחד ההסברים לכך שמצוות "הקהל" נקבעה בזמן האמור הוא: מאחר ושנת השמיטה היא "שבת לה'" שבה נוצל הזמן שבו היו חפשיים מעבודת שדה וכרם (שהיתה העיסוק העיקרי של האנשים באותן תקופות) להוסיף בלימוד התורה, בתפלה ובקיום המצוות במדה מוגברת — היתה זו ההכנה המתאימה וההכרחית לעליה לבית־המקדש כל בני ישראל כקהל אחד, ולהאזין לקריאת התורה כאילו היא נשמעת מפי הגבורה, תוך חוייה נשמתית עמוקה כבמתן תורה בהר סיני, דבר שנחקק עמוק בלב ובמוח והשתקף לאחר מכן בחיי יום יום במשך כל השנים הבאות.

Rabbi Menachem Mendel Schneerson
1902–1994
The towering Jewish leader of the 20th century, known as "the Lubavitcher Rebbe," or simply as "the Rebbe." Born in southern Ukraine, the Rebbe escaped Nazi-occupied Europe, arriving in the U.S. in June 1941. The Rebbe inspired and guided the revival of traditional Judaism after the European devastation, impacting virtually every Jewish community the world over. The Rebbe often emphasized that the performance of just one additional good deed could usher in the era of Mashiach. The Rebbe's scholarly talks and writings have been printed in more than 200 volumes.

One explanation given for the timing of the hakhel: *The* shemitah *year is year of rest, in which the people are free from working the fields and vineyards (which was the primary occupation of the Jewish people in those days). They therefore had time to increase their Torah study, prayer, and mitzvah observance to a great degree. Such behavior was appropriate and necessary for the Jewish people before traveling to the Temple together as one nation, to listen to the Torah read as if hearing it from G-d Himself, as part of a profound soulful experience, as was the case at Sinai. Such an experience would be engraved deep in the heart and mind, and would be reflected in day to day life for all coming years.*

Hakhel *Today*

TEXT 16

The Lubavitcher Rebbe, Letter dated 18 Elul 18 - Elul, 5712 [September 8, 1952]

To All My Brethren, Wherever You Are, G-d Bless You All.

Peace and blessing:

I send you herewith my prayerful wishes for a happy and pleasant New Year, may it bring blessings to us all.

At the end of this shemitah *(Sabbatical) Year, and on the threshold of the New Year, we are reminded of the great mitzvah, which is "a strong pillar and a great credit to our religion"—the mitzvah of* hakhel. *An even when all the people, men, women, and children gathered during the Festival of Sukkoth at the holy place in Jerusalem—may it be rebuilt by our righteous Messiah speedily in our rime—to hear selected portions of the Torah, portions inspiring to piety, love and appreciation of the Torah, the observance of the* mitzvot, *particularly the mitzvah of charity.*

Although at all times we are commanded to bring up our children in the way of the Torah and mitzvot, *the mitzvah of* hakhel, *coinciding with this season, impresses upon us our duties towards the children with especial force and timeliness.*

Therefore, let every Jewish father and mother, every Rabbi and leader, every communal worker and person of influence, heed the call of the mitzvah of hakhel: *to gather the masses of Jewish children and bring them to the Yeshivot, Talmud Torahs and Torah—true educational institutions; to increase the Torah-tzedakah, the support of true Torah institutions and ensure their existence and growth, in order that all Jewish children boys and girls be brought up in the spirit of piety and love for G-d, love for the Torah and* mitzvot, *and love for one another.*

In the merit of this, the Almighty will favor us and enable us very soon to fulfill the mitzvah of hakhel in the Temple in Jerusalem, rebuilt by our righteous Messiah, Amen.

With blessings to you and from you for a Happy and Pleasant Year, ksivah vachasimah tovah,

Menachem M. Schneerson

Pull Yourself Together

TEXT 17

The Lubavitcher Rebbe, Shaarei Hamoadim,
Shemini Atzeret-Simchat Torah, p. 374

עניינו של "הקהל", במובנו הרוחני, מזכיר ודורש מן האדם להקהיל ולאסוף את כל מחשבותיו, דיבוריו ומעשיו' ולרכזם ב"בית המקדש" הפנימי שלו, תוך התמסרות מלאה ומשמעת לדבר המלך—אל הקדוש ברוך הוא.

In a spiritual sense, hakhel *reminds us and demands from us to gather our thoughts, words, and actions, and concentrate them on our inner "Temple" out of complete devotion and fulfillment of G-d's words.*

10

ROSH HASHANAH

The Silent Voice

Listening to the Shofar's Call

*Dedicated in honor of the birth of **Chaya Mushka Piekarsky**.*
May she grow to be a source of continuous nachas and pride to her family and Klal Yisroel.

OVERVIEW
Rosh Hashanah

The festival of Rosh Hashanah—the name means "Head of the Year"—is observed for two days beginning on 1 Tishrei, the first day of the Jewish year. It is the anniversary of the creation of Adam and Eve, the first man and woman, and their first actions toward the realization of mankind's role in G-d's world.

Rosh Hashanah thus emphasizes the special relationship between G-d and humanity: our dependence upon G-d as our creator and sustainer, and G-d's dependence upon us as the ones who make His presence known and felt in His world. Each year on Rosh Hashanah, "all inhabitants of the world pass before G-d like a flock of sheep," and it is decreed in the heavenly court "who shall live, and who shall die . . . who shall be impoverished, and who shall be enriched; who shall fall and who shall rise." But this is also the day we proclaim G-d King of the Universe. The Kabbalists teach that the continued existence of the universe is dependent upon the renewal of the Divine desire for a world when we accept G-d's kingship each year on Rosh Hashanah.

The central observance of Rosh Hashanah is the sounding of the shofar, the ram's horn, which also represents the trumpet blast of a people's coronation of their king. The cry of the shofar is also a call to repentance, for Rosh Hashanah is also the anniversary of man's first sin and his repentance thereof, and serves as the first of the "Ten Days of Repentance" which culminate in Yom Kippur, the Day of Atonement. Another significance of the shofar is to recall the Binding of Isaac, which also occurred on Rosh Hashanah, in which a ram took Isaac's place as an offering to G-d; we evoke Abraham's readiness to sacrifice his son, and plead that the merit of his deed should stand by us as we pray for a year of life, health, and prosperity. Altogether, we listen to one hundred shofar blasts over the course of the Rosh Hashanah services.

Additional Rosh Hashanah observances include: a) Eating a piece of apple dipped in honey, to symbolize our desire for a sweet year, and other special foods symbolic of the new year's blessings. b) Blessing one another with the words "Leshanah tovah tikateiv veteichateim," "May you be inscribed and sealed for a good year." c) Tashlich, a special prayer said near a body of water (an ocean, river, pond, etc.), in evocation of the verse, "And You shall cast their sins into the depths of the sea." And as with every major Jewish holiday, after candlelighting and prayers we recite Kiddush and make a blessing on the challah.

Introduction

Mitzvah of the Day

TEXT 1

Bamidbar (Numbers) 29:1

וּבַחֹדֶשׁ הַשְּׁבִיעִי בְּאֶחָד לַחֹדֶשׁ מִקְרָא קֹדֶשׁ יִהְיֶה לָכֶם כָּל מְלֶאכֶת עֲבֹדָה לֹא תַעֲשׂוּ יוֹם תְּרוּעָה יִהְיֶה לָכֶם:

And in the seventh month, on the first day, there shall be a holy convocation for you; you shall not perform any mundane work. It shall be a day of shofar sounding for you.

TEXT 2

Talmud Tractate Rosh Hashanah, 26b

Babylonian Talmud
A literary work of monumental proportions that draws upon the legal, spiritual, intellectual, ethical, and historical traditions of Judaism. The 37 tractates of the Babylonian Talmud contain the teachings of the Jewish sages from the period after the destruction of the 2nd Temple through the 5th century CE. It has served as the primary vehicle for the transmission of the Oral Law and the education of Jews over the centuries; it is the entry point for all subsequent legal, ethical, and theological Jewish scholarship.

שופר של ראש השנה של יעל, פשוט ופיו מצופה זהב, ושתי חצוצרות מן הצדדין. שופר מאריך וחצוצרות מקצרות, שמצות היום בשופר.

The Rosh Hashanah shofar is the horn of an ibex, straight and [its mouthpiece] coated in gold, accompanied by two trumpets [one on each side of the one sounding the shofar]. Long blasts are blown with the

shofar, *while short blasts are blown with the trumpets,*
for the mitzvah of the day is the shofar [empha-
sis added].

Shofar Makes the Day

TEXT 3

The Lubavitcher Rebbe, Likutei Sichot vol. 34, p. 183

שכל ענייני ראש השנה נפעלים על ידי תקיעת שופר [וכנרמז גם
בלשון חז"ל "מצות היום בשופר", והיינו שתקיעת שופר היא
המצוה העיקרית דכל היום, כולל כל ענייני יום זה.]

The shofar blast effects all the proceedings of Rosh
Hashanah [as alluded to in the teaching of our Sages
that "The mitzvah of the day is the shofar," that is to
say, including all aspects of the day.]

**Rabbi Menachem
Mendel Schneerson**
1902–1994
The towering Jewish leader
of the 20th century, known
as "the Lubavitcher Rebbe,"
or simply as "the Rebbe."
Born in southern Ukraine,
the Rebbe escaped Nazi-
occupied Europe, arriving
in the U.S. in June 1941. The
Rebbe inspired and guided
the revival of traditional
Judaism after the European
devastation, impacting
virtually every Jewish
community the world over.
The Rebbe often emphasized
that the performance of
just one additional good
deed could usher in the era
of Mashiach. The Rebbe's
scholarly talks and writings
have been printed in more
than 200 volumes.

The Ten Reasons

TEXT 4

Rabbi David Abudraham, Sefer Abudraham,
Seder Tefillat Rosh Hashanah

**Rabbi David ben
Yoseph Abudraham**
14th century
Resided in Seville, Spain,
and is famous for his work on
Jewish prayers and blessings.
The work—completed
around the year 1340—is
a commentary on the
daily, Shabbat, and festival
prayers and collects many
customs and laws relating
to them. He is believed
to have been a disciple of
Rabbi Ya'akov ben Asher,
author of *Arba'ah Turim*.

כתב רבי סעדיה מה שצונו הבורא יתברך לתקוע בשופר בראש
השנה יש בזה עשרה ענינים. הענין הראשון מפני שהיום היתה
תחלת הבריאה שבו ברא הקדוש ברוך הוא את העולם ומלך עליו
וכן עושין המלכים בתחלת מלכותם שתוקעין לפניהם בחצוצרות
ובקרנות להודיע ולהשמיע בכל מקום התחלת מלכותם...

והענין הב' כי יום ראש השנה הוא ראשון לעשרת ימי תשובה
ותוקעין בו בשופר להכריז על ראשנו כמי שמזהיר ואומר כל הרוצה
לשוב ישוב ואם לאו אל יקרא תגר על עצמו. וכן עושין המלכים
מזהירין את העולם תחלה בגזירותם וכל העובר אחר האזהרה אין
שומעין לו טענה.

והענין השלישי להזכירנו מעמד הר סיני שנאמר בו "וקול שופר
חזק מאד". ונקבל על עצמינו מה שקבלו אבותינו על עצמם
נעשה ונשמע.

והענין הרביעי להזכירנו דברי הנביאים שנמשלו כתקיעת שופר
שנאמר "ושמע השומע את קול השופר ולא נזהר תבא חרב
ותקחהו דמו בראשו יהיה והוא נזהר נפשו מלט".

והענין הה' להזכירנו חרבן בית המקדש וקול תרועת מלחמת
האויבים כמו שנאמר "כי קול שופר שמעה נפשי תרועת מלחמה",
וכשאנו שומעים קול השופר נבקש מאת השם על בנין בית המקדש.

והענין הששי להזכירנו עקידת יצחק שמסר נפשו לשמים וכן אנחנו
נמסור נפשנו על קדושת שמו ויעלה זכרוננו לפניו לטובה.

ועניין השביעי כשנשמע תקיעת השופר נירא ונחרד ונשבר עצמנו
לפני הבורא. כי כך הוא טבע השופר מרעיד ומחריד כמו שנאמר
"אם יתקע שופר בעיר ועם לא יחרדו".

והעניין השמיני להזכיר יום הדין הגדול ולירא ממנו שנאמר בו "קרוב
יום ה' הגדול קרוב ומהר מאד יום שופר ותרועה".

ועניין הט' להזכירנו קבוץ נדחי ישראל ולהתאוות אליו שנאמר
בו "והיה ביום ההוא יתקע בשופר גדול ובאו האובדים בארץ
אשור וכו'".

והעניין הי' להזכירנו תחיית המתים ולהאמין בה שנאמר בה "כל
יושבי תבל ארץ כנשוא נס הרים תראו וכתקוע שופר תשמעו".

Rabbi Saadia Gaon recorded ten reasons for the com-
mandment to blow the shofar on Rosh Hashanah:

Rosh Hashanah marks the beginning of Creation,
when G-d created the world and proclaimed His rule
over it. It is customary to blow trumpets and horns to
publicize the beginning of a new monarch's reign…

Second, Rosh Hashanah marks the ten-day period of
repentance, so we blow the shofar as if to proclaim,
"Whoever wishes to repent, now is your chance.
Don't complain later if you miss it." This is analogous
to the way kings warn their subjects regarding their
decrees, so that if anyone transgresses them, there are
no excuses…

Third, the shofar reminds us of Mount Sinai… so that
we accept upon ourselves the commitment of our an-
cestors to keep and study the Torah.

Four: To remind us of the words of the Prophets, which are compared to the sound of the shofar…

Five: To remind us of the destruction of the Temple and the sound of the enemy's horn in battle, so that we beseech G-d to rebuild the Temple.

Six: To remind us of the binding of Isaac, who was willing to sacrifice his life to G-d [and only later was replaced with a ram], so that we, too, resolve to sacrifice our lives to G-d…

Seven: To fear G-d and tremble and submit ourselves before Him, for by nature the shofar blast inspires fear and awe…

Eight: To remember the great Day of Judgment and fear G-d…

Nine: To remind us of and cause us to yearn for the Ingathering of the Exiles, when the "Great Shofar will be blown, and the lost ones in the Land of Assyria will come, etc."

Ten: To remind us of and renew our faith in the Revival of the Dead, as the verse states, "All inhabitants of the world and dwellers of the earth, when a standard of the mountains is raised you shall see, and when a shofar is sounded you shall hear."

The Battle Cry

TEXT 5

Rabbi Aharon Halevi of Barcelona, Sefer Hachinuch, Mitzvat Shofar

לפי שהאדם בעל חומר, לא יתעורר לדברים כי אם על יד מעורר,
כדרך בני אדם בעת מלחמה יריעו כדי שיתעורר למלחמה. וגם כן
ביום ראש השנה שהוא היום לדון כל באי עולם... השופר מעורר
הרבה לב שומעיו, העומדים לפני ה' במשפט לחיים, או ח"ו למוות.

**Rabbi Aharon Halevi
of Barcelona
(Re'ah)**
1235–1290
Born in Gerona, Spain. Rabbi,
talmudist, and authority on
Jewish law. Rabbi Aharon
studied under Nachmanides
and under his father,
Rabbi Yosef Halevi, and
corresponded with the leading
talmudic scholars of his
generation. His explanations
on the Rashba's halachic
code, *Torat Habayit*, entitled
Bedek Habayit, are integral
in the formation of Jewish
law. Rabbi Aharon was
considered by some to be the
anonymous author of *Sefer
Hachinuch*, a compendium
of the 613 commandments.

As a corporeal entity, a human being will only be inspired if someone or something triggers that inspiration. Indeed, we find that trumpets are blown to rally the troops in times of war. Similarly, on Rosh Hashanah, the Day of Judgment for all creatures, the shofar blast arouses the hearts of those who hear it, as they stand before G-d in judgment of life or, G-d forbid, death.

The Wake-up Call

TEXT 6

Maimonides, Laws of Teshuvah, 3:4

**Rabbi Moshe
ben Maimon**
(Maimonides, Rambam)
1135–1204

Halachist, philosopher, author,
and physician. Maimonides
was born in Cordoba, Spain.
After the conquest of Cordoba
by the Almohads, he fled
Spain and eventually settled
in Cairo, Egypt. There, he
became the leader of the
Jewish community and served
as court physician to the vizier
of Egypt. He is most noted
for authoring the *Mishneh
Torah*, an encyclopedic
arrangement of Jewish law,
and for his philosophical
work, *Guide for the Perplexed*.
His rulings on Jewish law
are integral to the formation
of halachic consensus.

אַף-עַל-פִּי שתקיעת שופר בראש השנה גזירת הכתוב היא רמז
יש בו: עורו ישנים משנתכם ונרדמים הקיצו מתרדמתכם וחפשו
מעשיכם וחזרו בתשובה וזכרו בוראכם. אלו השוכחים את האמת
בהבלי הזמן ושוגים כל שנתם בהבל וריק אשר לא יועיל ולא יציל
הביטו לנפשותיכם והטיבו דרכיכם ומעלליכם ויעזוב כל אחד מכם
דרכו הרעה ומחשבתו אשר לא טובה.

*Even though the sounding of the shofar on Rosh Ha-
shanah is a decree, it contains an allusion. It is as if
[the shofar's call] is saying: Wake up, you sleepy ones,
from your sleep, and you who slumber, arise. Inspect
your deeds, repent, remember your Creator. Those who
forget the truth in the vanities of time and throughout
the entire year, devote their energies to vanity and
emptiness that will not benefit or save: Look to your
souls. Improve your ways and your deeds and let every
one of you abandon his evil path and thoughts.*

Two Parables

The Wandering Prince

TEXT 7

Rabbi Yisrael Baal Shem Tov, Keter Shem Tov, Appendix Sec. 194

ונתבאר משל על זה בשם הבעל שם טוב ז"ל למלך שהיה לו בן
יחיד מלומד היטב שהיה חביב אצלו כבבת עינו ממש, ועלה בדעת
האב ובנו שיסע למדינות אחרות ללמוד חכמות ולידע הנהגת בני
אדם, אז נתן לו אביו המלך שרים ומשרתים והון רב שילך ויתור
במדינות ואיי הים למען יגיע הבן למעלה יתירה יותר מכמו היותו
אצל אביו בביתו.

ויהי ברבות הימים וכל אשר נתן לו אביו הלך על הוצאות הדרך
מהצטרכות תפנוקיו שהיה מורגל, והעיקר במה שהוסיף תאווה על
תאוותו . . עד שמכר כל אשר לו, ובין כך הלך למדינה רחוקה עד
שגם אביו לא נודע שם כלל . .

בצר לו, עלה בלבו לחזור למדינת אביו, אבל מחמת אריכות הזמן
שכח גם לשון מדינתו, ובבואו למדינתו מה יכול לעשות מאחר שגם
הלשון שכח. והתחיל לרמז להם שהוא בן מלכם . . עד שהגיע לחצר
המלך והתחיל לרמז להם שהוא בן המלך ולא השגיחו עליו כלום.
עד שהתחיל לצעוק בקול גדול בכדי שיכיר המלך קולו, וכשהכיר
המלך קולו אמר הלא זה זהו קול בני צועק מתוך דוחקו ונתעורר אצלו
אהבת בנו וחבקו ונשקו כו'.

*The Baal Shem Tov explained [the call of the shofar]
with the following parable: There was once a king who
had a very knowledgeable son who was very dear to*

**Rabbi Yisrael
Baal Shem Tov**
(Besht)
1698–1760
Founder of the Chasidic
movement. Born in Slutsk,
Belarus, the Baal Shem Tov
was orphaned as a child.
He served as a teacher's
assistant and clay digger
before founding the Chasidic
movement and revolutionizing
the Jewish world with his
emphasis on prayer, joy,
and love for every Jew,
regardless of his or her
level of Torah knowledge.

him, as the apple of his eye. The king decided that the prince should travel to foreign lands to learn from their wisdom and customs. The king provided the prince with officers and servants and a vast amount of money, enabling him to tour foreign lands and islands, so that he would grow more cultured than he would at home.

As time passed, the prince wasted all the money his father had given him on the various luxuries he was accustomed to, even indulging more than he typically would at home… Eventually, he was forced to sell everything he owned, and in the process ended up in a place so far away that the inhabitants had never even heard of his father…

In his distress, the prince decided to return home, but after traveling for such an extended period of time, he no longer even remembered how to speak his native language. When he arrived in his homeland, the prince was at a loss, for he couldn't even communicate in the local tongue. Using various motions and hints, he began to indicate that he was the prince… until he arrived at the palace courtyard and tried to show that he was the prince. But nobody paid any attention to him.

At that point, the prince finally began to cry out loud, in the hope that his father would recognize his voice. When the king heard the prince's voice, he recognized his son calling out in distress, and his love for his son was stirred, and he hugged and kissed him, etc.

TEXT 8

Ibid, ad loc.

וכך יובן הנמשל למעלה, שנשמות ישראל נקראים בנים למקום . . והוריד הנשמה בגוף, שזהו כמשל בן המלך שהלך בדרך רחוקה בכדי להתלמד, היינו שעל ידי מצות ומעשים טובים על ידי זה מתעלים הנשמות בעילוי יותר נעלה מכמו שהיה מקודם, ואמנם, על ידי אהבת הגוף ותאוות . . נתרחק מאד למקום שאינו יכול כלל שם אביו . . ששכח גם הלשון . . עד שהתחיל לשוב ולצעוק בקול פשוט . .

וזהו התקיעה בקול שופר, שהוא בחינת צעקה פנימית מעומקא דלבא איך שהוא מתחרט על העבר ומקבל על עצמו להבא לשמוע בקול אביו, ועל ידי צעקה זו מתעורר מלך מלכי המלכים הקדוש ברוך הוא ומראה חיבתו לבנו יחידו ומוחל וסולח לו על העבר כו'.

So it is in the analogue: Jewish souls are called G-d's children... Now, the soul descends to this world in a body, just like the prince who traveled to faraway lands to learn. The analogy is that through observing the mitzvot and doing good deeds, a soul is elevated far higher than its level before it descended [similar to the prince who was supposed to become more cultured from his travels].

Alas, out of love for the body and physical passion, [it can happen that] the soul becomes very far removed, to the point that it no longer recognizes G-d's Name, and doesn't even know its own language…until finally it starts to return and call out with a simple cry…

This, then, is the symbolism of the simple shofar blast, which represents the inner call from the depths of the heart, coming from regret for the past and a resolve to listen to his father. This call arouses G-d to show His love for His only child and forgive him for the past, etc.

The Wise Man Who Sinned

TEXT 9

Rabbi Levi Yitzchak of Berditchev, Kedushat Levi, Derush L'Rosh Hashanah, s.v. Bachatzotzrot

Rabbi Levi Yitzchak of Berditchev
1740–1809
Chasidic rebbe. Rabbi Levi Yitzchak was one of the foremost disciples of the Magid of Mezeritch and later went on to serve as rabbi in Berditchev, Ukraine. His Chasidic commentary on the Torah, *Kedushat Levi*, is a classic that is popular to this day. He is known in Jewish history and folklore for his all-encompassing love, compassion, and advocacy on behalf of the Jewish people.

מלך בשר ודם שנסע ליער גדול . . עד שבא לעומק היער ולא מצא הדרך הנכון והישר לשוב לביתו, וראה ביער אנשים כפרים ושאלם על הדרך, ולא הכירו את המלך, ולא ידעו מה להשיב לו כי מעולם לא ידעו את דרך המלך הגדול הנכון והישר.

עד שמצא איש חכם ונבון, אז הבין החכם שהמלך הוא, ונזדעזע לאחוריו, ושמע תיכף לרצונו, ויראתו את הדרך, כי מרוב חכמתו ידע את הדרך המלך הנכון והישר, ויולך את המלך לבית המלוכה ויושב אותו על כסא מלכותו אשר בבית המלכות וימצא האיש ההוא חן . .

ויהי אחרי ימים רבים חטא אותו האיש למלך, ויקצוף עליו המלך, ויצו לשרים היושבים ראשונה במלכות לשפוט אותו האיש כדין העובר על מצות המלך. ויצר להאיש מאד, כי ידע משפטו יהיה חרוץ לרע לו על דבר אשר חטא נגד המלך.

ויפול לפני המלך ויבקש על נפשו, שקודם שיצא דבר משפטו, ימלא שאלתו בדבר א', והוא, להלביש אותו בגדים הראשונים שלו בשעה שהוליך את המלך מהיער, וגם המלך ילבוש בגדים שלבש אז. וישא לו המלך לדבר הזה.

ויהי כאשר לבש המלך את בגדיו הנ"ל והאיש את בגדיו הנ"ל, זכר המלך את גודל החסד שעשה עמו אשר החזיר אותו לבית המלוכה וישיבתו על כסא מלכותו, ויכמרו רחמיו עליו, וימצא חן וחסד לפניו, והעביר את חטאתו מלפניו, והשיבהו על כנו.

A parable is given of a king who got lost in the forest, unable to find his way home. In the forest he saw some townsfolk, and he asked them for directions. But they didn't recognize him as the king, and did not know what to tell him, for they had never in their lives seen the great road leading directly to the palace.

Eventually, the king met a wise man and asked him the way. The wise man understood that standing before him was the king, and he drew back in respect and immediately fulfilled the king's wish by showing him the way, for in his great wisdom he was familiar with the great road leading directly to the palace. He led the king back to the palace and back to his throne.

Many years later, this wise man committed an offense against the king. Enraged, the king commanded his chief ministers to sentence him as befitting one who transgresses the king's decree. The man was greatly troubled, for he knew he would be punished gravely.

He fell before the king and begged that the king grant him one wish: That he be permitted to wear the same clothes he wore on the day he led the king back to his palace from the forest, and that the king likewise wear the same clothes he wore that day. The king granted his wish.

When they both wore their respective clothing, the king remembered the great kindness this wise man had done in returning him to his palace and his throne. His mercy was aroused, and the wise man found favor in his eyes. The king thus forgave the offense and set the man free.

TEXT 10

Ibid, ad loc.

ככל המשל הזה כן אנחנו בני ישראל, בשעת מתן תורה החזיר
הקדוש ברוך הוא התורה על כל אומה ולשון ולא קבלוה, ואנחנו בני
ישראל קבלנו התורה בשמחה ועונג עד אשר קדמנו נעשה לנשמע,
וקבלנו עול מלכות שמים ונמליכו למלך עלינו, לקיים מצותיו וחוקיו
ותורתו הקדושה, ועתה פשענו ומרדנו נגדו . .
לכן אנחנו תוקעים בשופר היינו באותו הלבוש שהיה במתן תורה,
בכדי שיזכור שקבלנו התורה והמלכנו אותו בשופר, כמו שכתוב
"ויהי קול השופר" . . ועל ידי זכרון זכות זה מוחל לנו על כל
עוונותינו, ויכתבנו לחיים טובים לאלתר כו'".

*This is the analogue: Before the Torah was given, G-d
offered it to each and every nation, but none of them
accepted. However, we the Jewish people accepted it
with joy, agreeing to observe it before even knowing
what it contained. We accepted upon ourselves the yoke
of G-d's kingdom, and crowned Him as King upon us,
to fulfill His commandments and His holy Torah. But
now we have sinned and rebelled against Him…*

*Therefore we blow the shofar—which is like the "cloth-
ing" we "wore" at Sinai, so that G-d will remember
how we accepted the Torah and crowned Him our King
with shofar blasts, as the verse states, "The sound of
the shofar"… Upon remembering this merit of ours,
G-d forgives us for all our sins, and inscribes us for a
good life immediately.*

The Core of Rosh Hashanah

The Musaf *Verses*

TEXT 11

Talmud Tractate Rosh Hashanah, 32b

אמר רבה, אמר הקדוש ברוך הוא: אמרו לפני בראש השנה מלכיות זכרונות ושופרות. מלכיות—כדי שתמליכוני עליכם, זכרונות—כדי שיבא לפני זכרוניכם לטובה, ובמה—בשופר.

Rabbah said: G-d says, "On Rosh Hashanah, recite before Me verses describing kingship, verses describing remembrance, and verses describing the shofar blast. Kingship—so as to crown Me as your King. Remembrance—so that you be remembered before Me for good. With what [shall you crown me as King and be remembered before Me for good]? With the shofar."

What the Shofar Says

TEXT 12

The Lubavitcher Rebbe, Likutei Sichot vol. 34, p. 185

ועל פי זה מובן הפירוש ד"ובמה בשופר," שב' הענינים ד"תמליכוני
עליכם" ו"יבא לפני זכרוניכם לטובה", נעשים בפועלה על ידי
השופר - שהרי השופר הוא דוגמת הצעקה בקול פשוט ("תמליכוני
עליכם"), וכן דוגמת הלבוש שהיה בשעת מתן תורה ("יבא לפני
זכרוניכם לטובה"), כמובן מב' משלים אלה.

The shofar effects both the "Crown me as King" and the "Be remembered before Me for good" aspects of Rosh Hashanah. For the shofar is analogous to the simple call from the depths of the soul, and is likewise analogous to the "garment" the Jewish people wore when they received the Torah, as is understood from these two parables.

The Simple Meaning of Rosh Hashanah

TEXT 13

The Lubavitcher Rebbe, Likutei Sichot vol. 4, p. 1145

אין וואס באשטייט די עבודה פון ראש השנה שמצד עצמו—"אמרו
לפני כו' מלכיות כדי שתמליכוני עליכם".

At its core, the main thrust of what Rosh Hashanah is all about is [as the Talmud states,] "Recite before Me verses describing Kingship… so as to crown Me as your King."

YOM KIPPUR

The Holy Heretic

All Is Never Lost

Dedicated in honor of the birth of **Zelda Rochel Sirota**.
May she grow to be a source of continuous nachas and pride to her family and Klal Yisroel.

OVERVIEW
Yom Kippur

Yom Kippur is the holiest day of the year—the day on which we are closest to G-d and to the quintessence of our own souls. It is the Day of Atonement—"For on this day He will forgive you, to purify you, that you be cleansed from all your sins before G-d" (Leviticus 16:30).

For nearly twenty-six hours—from several minutes before sunset on 9 Tishrei to after nightfall on 10 Tishrei—we "afflict our souls": we abstain from food and drink, do not wash or anoint our bodies, do not wear leather footwear, and abstain from marital relations.

Before Yom Kippur we perform the kaparot *atonement service; we request and receive honey cake, in acknowledgement that we are all recipients in G-d's world, and in prayerful hope for a sweet and abundant year; eat a festive meal; immerse in a* mikvah; *and give extra charity. In the late afternoon we eat the pre-fast meal, following which we bless our children, light a memorial candle as well as the holiday candles, and go to the synagogue for the Kol Nidrei service.*

In the course of Yom Kippur we hold five prayer services: Maariv, *with its solemn* Kol Nidrei *service, on the eve of Yom Kippur;* Shacharit—*the morning prayer, which includes a reading from Leviticus followed by the Yizkor memorial service;* Musaf, *which includes a detailed account of the Yom Kippur Temple service;* Minchah, *which includes the reading of the Book of Jonah; and* Neilah, *the "closing of the gates" service at sunset. We say the* Al Chet *confession of sins eight times in the course of Yom Kippur, and recite Psalms every available moment.*

The day is the most solemn of the year, yet an undertone of joy suffuses it: a joy that revels in the spirituality of the day and expresses the confidence that G-d will accept our repentance, forgive our sins, and seal our verdict for a year of life, health and happiness. The closing Neilah *service climaxes in the resounding cries of "Hear O Israel . . . G-d is one." Then joy erupts in song and dance (a Chabad custom is to sing the lively "Napoleon's March"), followed by a single blast of the* shofar, *followed by the proclamation, "Next year in Jerusalem." We then partake of a festive after-fast meal, making the evening after Yom Kippur a* yom tov *(festival) in its own right.*

The Tragic Story of Elisha ben Abuya

Bright Beginnings

TEXT 1

Cited as Midrash Ruth Rabah, 6:4

Ruth Rabah
A Midrashic text on the Book of Ruth. *Midrash* is the designation of a particular genre of rabbinic literature. The term Midrash is derived from the root *d-r-sh* (*dalet-raish-shin*), which means "to search," "to examine," and "to investigate." This particular Midrash provides textual exegeses, expounds upon the biblical narrative of Ruth, and develops and illustrates moral principles. It was first printed in Pesaro, Italy, in 1519, together with four other Midrashic works on the other four biblical *megilot*.

אָמְרוּ עָלָיו עַל אֱלִישָׁע בֶּן אֲבוּיָה, שֶׁלֹּא הָיְתָה הָעֲזָרָה נִנְעֶלֶת עַל אִישׁ חָכָם וְגִבּוֹר בַּתּוֹרָה בְּיִשְׂרָאֵל כְּמוֹתוֹ, וְכֵיוָן שֶׁהָיָה מְדַבֵּר וְדוֹרֵשׁ בְּלִשְׁכַּת הַגָּזִית אוֹ בְּבֵית הַמִּדְרָשׁ שֶׁל טְבֶרְיָא, הָיוּ כָל הַחֲבֵרִים עוֹמְדִים וּמַאֲזִינִים לִדְבָרָיו, וְאַחַר כָּךְ בָּאִים כֻּלָּם וְנוֹשְׁקִין אוֹתוֹ עַל רֹאשׁוֹ. אִם בִּטְבֶרְיָא כָּךְ, קַל וָחֹמֶר בִּשְׁאָר מְדִינוֹת וּבִשְׁאָר עֲיָרוֹת.

It was said about Elisha ben Abuya that the gates of the Azarah were never closed before such a wise and mighty man of Torah. When he would expound in Torah in the Chamber of Hewn Stone [in the Temple] or in the study hall of Tiberias, all his colleagues would stand and listen to his words. Thereafter, they would all approach him and kiss him on his head. If this was the situation in Tiberias [a scholarly town], certainly it was so in other countries and cities.

Things Turn Sour

TEXT 2

Talmud Tractate Chagigah, 15a

נפק אחר לתרבות רעה. נפק אשכח זונה, תבעה. אמרה ליה: ולאו
אלישע בן אבויה את? - עקר פוגלא ממישרא בשבת ויהב לה.
אמרה: אחר הוא.

Acher gave himself over to evil ways. He found a prostitute and propositioned her. She said, "But aren't you the famous Elisha ben Abuyah?"

He plucked a radish out of its bed on Shabbat, and gave it to her. She said, "You are Acher—the Other One." [And that is how he came to be called Acher.]

Babylonian Talmud
A literary work of monumental proportions that draws upon the legal, spiritual, intellectual, ethical, and historical traditions of Judaism. The 37 tractates of the Babylonian Talmud contain the teachings of the Jewish sages from the period after the destruction of the 2nd Temple through the 5th century CE. It has served as the primary vehicle for the transmission of the Oral Law and the education of Jews over the centuries; it is the entry point for all subsequent legal, ethical, and theological Jewish scholarship.

TEXT 3

Jerusalem Talmud Tractate Chagigah, 2:1

Jerusalem Talmud

A commentary to the Mishnah, compiled during the 4th and 5th centuries. The Jerusalem Talmud predates its Babylonian counterpart by 100 years and is written in both Hebrew and Aramaic. While the Babylonian Talmud is the most authoritative source for Jewish law, the Jerusalem Talmud remains an invaluable source for the spiritual, intellectual, ethical, historical, and legal traditions of Judaism.

אחר הציץ וקיצץ בנטיעות מני אחר אלישע בן אבויה שהיה הורג
רבי תורה אמרין כל תלמיד דהוה חמי ליה משכח באוריתא הוה
קטיל ליה.

ולא עוד אלא דהוה עליל לבית וועדא והוה חמי טלייא קומי ספרא
והוה אמר מה אילין יתבין עבדין הכא אומנותיה דהן בנאי אומנותיה
דהן נגר אומנותיה דהן צייד אומנותיה דהן חייט וכיון דהוון שמעין
כן הוון שבקין ליה ואזלין לון.

"Acher *saw and mutilated the shoots." Who is* Acher?" *It is Elisha ben Abuya who would murder Torah scholars. It is said that he would murder any scholar whom he witnessed studying Torah.*

What's more, when he entered a meeting place of scholars and saw youngsters with scrolls in front of them, he would say, "Why do they sit here and occupy themselves in this manner? This one's craft should be that of a builder. This one's, that of a carpenter. That one's, that of a painter. And that other one's, that of a tailor." When the youngsters heard such talk, they left their scrolls and went away.

A Disastrous Journey
into the Orchard

TEXT 4A

Tractate Chagigah, loc cit., 14b

תנו רבנן: ארבעה נכנסו בפרדס. ואלו הם: בן עזאי ובן זומא, אחר
ורבי עקיבא... בן עזאי הציץ ומת... בן זומא הציץ ונפגע... אחר
קיצץ בנטיעות, רבי עקיבא יצא בשלום.

Our rabbis taught: "Four men entered a garden: Ben Azzai, Ben Zoma, 'the Other One,' and Rabbi Akiba. ... Ben Azzai looked and perished. ... Ben Zoma looked and went mad. ... Acher mutilated the young plants. Rabbi Akiba came out safely."

TEXT 4B

Ibid. 15a

אחר קיצץ בנטיעות... מאי היא? חזא מיטטרון דאתיהבא ליה
רשותא למיתב למיכתב זכוותא דישראל, אמר: גמירא דלמעלה לא
הוי לא ישיבה ולא תחרות ולא עורף ולא עיפוי, שמא חס ושלום
שתי רשויות הן.

אפקוהו למיטטרון ומחיוהו שיתין פולסי דנורא. אמרו ליה: מאי
טעמא כי חזיתיה לא קמת מקמיה? איתיהיבא ליה רשותא למימחק
זכוותא דאחר.

יצתה בת קול ואמרה "שובו בנים שובבים" - חוץ מאחר, אמר: הואיל
ואיטריד ההוא גברא מההוא עלמא ליפוק ליתהני בהאי עלמא.

*"Acher mutilated the shoots."… What does it refer
to? — He saw that permission was granted to the
angel Metatron to sit down one hour each day, while
he recorded the merits of the Jewish people. [He was
shocked, since he had expected that in heaven only
G-d is seated, while the other heavenly beings stand in
attendance on Him.] He said … "Perhaps (G-d forbid)
there are two divinities!"*

*Thereupon [the other angels] took Metatron outside
and gave him sixty lashes with a whip made of fire.
"Why didn't you stand up when you saw him?"
they demanded. Afterwards, Metatron was given
permission to erase from his book the merits of "the
Other One."*

A heavenly voice proclaimed, "Repent, you backsliding children—except for Acher." He said, "Since I have been banished from that world, let me go out and enjoy this world.

Foreign Interests

TEXT 5

Ibid. 15b

"אחר" מאי? (מפני מה בא לידי כך ולא הגנה תורתו עליו? –רש"י) זמר יווני לא פסיק מפומיה. אמרו עליו, על אחר: בשעה שהיה עומד מבית המדרש, הרבה ספרי מינין נושרין מחיקו.

But what of Acher? (I.e., why did not his Torah study save him? –Rashi) Greek song did not cease from his mouth. It is told of Acher that when he used to rise [to go] from the schoolhouse, many heretical books used to fall from his lap.

Harsh Reality

TEXT 6A

Jerusalem Talmud loc. cit

וכל דא מן הן אתת ליה?

אלא, פעם אחת היה יושב ושונה בבקעת גיניסר וראה אדם אחד עלה לראש הדקל ונטל אם על הבנים וירד משם בשלום. למחר ראה אדם אחר שעלה לראש הדקל ונטל את הבנים ושילח את האם וירד משם והכישו נחש ומת. אמר: כתיב "שלח תשלח את האם ואת הבנים תקח לך למען ייטב לך והארכת ימים". איכן היא טובתו של זה איכן היא אריכות ימיו של זה?

ולא היה יודע שדרשה רבי יעקב לפנים ממנו: למען ייטב לך לעולם הבא שכולו טוב, והארכת ימים לעתיד שכולו ארוך.

How did Elisha fall into heresy?

It once happened that he was sitting studying in the valley of Gennesaret. He saw a man climb to the top of a tree [where there was a bird's nest containing a mother and her chicks]. The man took both the mother and her chicks, and climbed down safely. The next day he saw another man climb to the top of a tree, take the chicks only, and release the mother. When the man reached the ground, a snake bit him and he died. Elisha recalled that the verse states, "You must certainly set the mother free, and take only the chicks. Thus you will have a good life and a long one." What happened, he wondered, to this man's good life? What happened to his long life?

Unfortunately, Elisha was not aware of the interpretation Rabbi Jacob had already given the passage: Thus you will have a good life—in the next world, which is entirely good. And a long one—in the future life, where everything lasts long. [And so he fell into heresy.]

TEXT 6B

Ibid.

> ויש אומרים על ידי שראה לשונו של רבי יהודה הנחתום נתון בפי
> הכלב שותת דם. אמר זו תורה וזו שכרה זהו הלשון שהיה מוציא
> דברי תורה כתיקנן זה הוא הלשון שהיה יגיע בתורה כל ימיו זו
> תורה וזו שכרה?! דומה שאין מתן שכר ואין תחיית המתים.

Others tell a different story. Once, Elisha saw in a dog's mouth the tongue of Rabbi Judah the Baker, dripping blood. "This is the Torah," he said, "and this is its reward? This is the tongue that faithfully declared the Torah's words? This is the tongue that never tired of speaking Torah? This is the Torah, and this is its reward? Clearly enough, there is no reward and there is no resurrection."

In His Youth

TEXT 7A

Ibid.

וּבִי הָיָה הַמַּעֲשֶׂה: אֲבוּיָה אַבָּא מִגְּדוֹלֵי יְרוּשָׁלַם הָיָה. בַּיּוֹם שֶׁבָּא
לְמוֹהֲלֵינִי קָרָא לְכָל גְּדוֹלֵי יְרוּשָׁלַם וְהוֹשִׁיבָן בְּבַיִת אֶחָד וְלר' אֱלִיעֶז'
וְלר' יְהוֹשֻׁעַ בְּבַיִת אַחֵר. מִן דְּאָכְלוֹן וְשָׁתוֹן, שָׁרוֹן מְטַפְּחִין וּמְרַקְדְּקִין.
אָ"ר לִיעֶזֶר לר' יְהוֹשֻׁעַ: עַד דְּאִינּוּן עֲסִיקִין בְּדִידוֹן נֵעֲסוֹק אֲנַן בְּדִידָן.
וְיָשְׁבוּ וְנִתְעַסְּקוּ בְּדִבְרֵי תוֹרָה מִן הַתּוֹרָה לַנְּבִיאִים וּמִן הַנְּבִיאִי'
לַכְּתוּבִים וְיָרְדָה אֵשׁ מִן הַשָּׁמַיִם וְהִקִּיפָה אוֹתָם. אָמַר לָהֶן אֲבוּיָה:
רַבּוֹתַי, מָה בָּאתֶם לִשְׂרוֹף אֶת בֵּיתִי עֲלַי! אָמְרוּ לוֹ: חַס וְשָׁלוֹם, אֶלָּא
יוֹשְׁבִין הָיִינוּ וְחוֹזְרִין בְּדִבְרֵי תוֹר' מִן הַתּוֹרָה לַנְּבִיאִים וּמִן הַנְּבִיאִים
לַכְּתוּבִים, וְהָיוּ הַדְּבָרִים שְׂמֵחִים כִּנְתִינָתָן מִסִּינַי וְהָיִת' הָאֵשׁ מְלַחֲכ'
אוֹתָן כִּלְחִיכָתָן מִסִּינַי, וְעִיקַּר נְתִינָתָן מִסִּינַי לֹא נִיתְּנוּ אֶלָּא בָּאֵשׁ, וְהָהָר
בּוֹעֵר בָּאֵשׁ עַד לֵב הַשָּׁמַיִם. אָמ' לָהֶן אֲבוּיָה אַבָּא: רַבּוֹתַי, אִם כָּךְ הִיא
כּוֹחָהּ שֶׁל תּוֹרָה, אִם נִתְקַיֵּים לִי בֵּן הַזֶּה, לַתּוֹרָה אֲנִי מַפְרִישׁוֹ. לְפִי
שֶׁלֹּא הָיְתָה כַּוָּונָתוֹ לְשֵׁם שָׁמַיִם, לְפִיכָךְ לֹא נִתְקַיְּימוּ בְּאוֹתוֹ הָאִישׁ.

So it happened with me. Abuyah, my father, was one of the notables of Jerusalem. When he was arranging for my circumcision, he invited all the notables of Jerusalem, among them Rabbi Eliezer and Rabbi Yehoshuah. After the crown had eaten and drunk, they began to clap their hands and dance. Some of the notables sang songs, and others composed alphabetical acrostics. Rabbi Eliezer said to Rabbi Yehoshuah: These are occupied with what interests them; shall we not occupy ourselves with what interests us? They began to speak words of Torah, and from the Torah to the Prophets, and from the Prophets to the Writings. And fire came down from heaven and surrounded them. At that point Abuyah said to them: My masters, have you come to set my house afire over me? They replied: G-d forbid! We were merely sitting and stringing words of Torah, then from the Torah we went on to the Prophets, and from the Prophets to the Writings. The words were as joyful as when they were given at Sinai. For when originally given at Sinai, they were given in the midst of fire, as is said, "The mountain burned with fire unto the heart of heaven." Elated, my father Abuyah remarked, "My masters, since the power of Torah is so great, if this child stays alive for me, I will dedicate him to the Torah." But because the intent of my father's resolve was not for the sake of Heaven, my study of Torah did not endure with me.

TEXT 7B

Ibid.

ויש אומרים: אמו, כשהיתה מעוברת בו, היתה עוברת על בתי
עבודה זרה והריחה מאותו המין, והיה אותו הריח מפעפע בגופה
כאירסה של חכינה.

And some say that his mother passed by a pagan temple while she was pregnant with him. The smell of the pagan sacrifices entered her nostrils and spread through her body like a snake's venom.

Denied Entry

The Shabbat Stroll

TEXT 8A

Talmud Tractate Chagigah, 15a

מעשה באחר שהיה רוכב על הסוס בשבת, והיה רבי מאיר מהלך
אחריו ללמוד תורה מפיו. אמר לו: מאיר, חזור לאחריך, שכבר
שיערתי בעקבי סוסי עד כאן תחום שבת. אמר ליה: אף אתה חזור
בך. - אמר ליה: ולא כבר אמרתי לך: כבר שמעתי מאחורי הפרגוד
שובו בנים שובבים - חוץ מאחר.

*Our rabbis taught: It once happened that Acher was
riding his horse on the Sabbath, while Rabbi Meir
walked after him to learn Torah from him. "Meir,"
he said, "turn back. I calculate from my horse's paces
that we have reached the Shabbat limit." Meir said,
"You too—turn back!" "Haven't I already told you?"
he said. "I have already heard from behind the veil,
'Repent, you backsliding children—except for Acher.'"*

TEXT 8B

Jerusalem Talmud loc. cit

אמר ליה דייך מאיר עד כאן תחום שבת.

אמר ליה מן הן את ידע?

אמר ליה מן טלפי דסוסיי דהוינא מני והולך אלפיים אמה.

אמר ליה וכל הדא חכמתא אית בך ולית את חזר בך?!

אמר ליה לית אנא יכיל.

אמר ליה למה?

אמר ליה שפעם אחת הייתי עובר לפני בית קודש הקדשים רכוב
על סוסי ביום הכיפורים שחל להיות בשבת ושמעתי בת קול יוצאת
מבית קודש הקדשים ואומרת שובו בנים חוץ מאלישע בן אבויה
שידע כחי ומרד בי.

"That's enough, Meir," he said. "We have now reached
the Sabbath limit."

"How do you know?"

"I calculated from the paces of my horse that we have
gone 2000 cubits."

"You have all this wisdom," said Meir, "and yet you do
not repent?!"

"I can't."

"Why not?"

"Once, I was riding my horse in front of the Holy of
Holies, on the Day of Atonement, which happened to
fall on a Sabbath. I heard the Divine voice issue from

the Holy of Holies, 'Repent, you backsliding children—
except for Elisha ben Abuyah, who knew My power
and rebelled against Me.'"

What Happened to Teshuvah?

TEXT 9

Midrash Tehillim, ch. 65

שערי תשובה אינן ננעלין לעולם, שנאמר "מבטח כל קצוי ארץ
וים רחוקים", מה הים הזה אינו ננעל לעולם, וכל מי שהוא מבקש
לרחוץ בו, רוחץ בו כל שעה שירצה, כך התשובה כל שעה שאדם
רוצה לעשות תשובה הקדוש ברוך הוא מקבל.

Midrash Tehillim
A rabbinic commentary on the
Book of Psalms. Midrash is
the designation of a particular
genre of rabbinic literature
usually forming a running
commentary on specific books
of the Bible. This particular
Midrash provides textual
exegeses and develops and
illustrates the principles
of the Book of Psalms.

The gates of teshuvah *are never closed, as it is stated,*
"[G-d of our salvation], the trust of all the distant
ends of the earth and the sea." Just as the sea is never
closed, always available for those who wish to bathe in
her waters, so it is with teshuvah: *Whenever one does*
teshuvah, *G-d accepts it.*

TEXT 10

Maimonides, Mishneh Torah, Laws of Teshuvah 3:14

**Rabbi Moshe
ben Maimon**
(Maimonides, Rambam)
1135–1204
Halachist, philosopher, author,
and physician. Maimonides
was born in Cordoba, Spain.
After the conquest of Cordoba
by the Almohads, he fled
Spain and eventually settled
in Cairo, Egypt. There, he
became the leader of the
Jewish community and served
as court physician to the vizier
of Egypt. He is most noted
for authoring the *Mishneh
Torah*, an encyclopedic
arrangement of Jewish law,
and for his philosophical
work, *Guide for the Perplexed*.
His rulings on Jewish law
are integral to the formation
of halachic consensus.

אין לך דבר שעומד בפני התשובה, אפילו כפר בעיקר כל ימיו
ובאחרונה שב יש לו חלק לעולם הבא, שנאמר "שלום שלום
לרחוק ולקרוב אמר ה' ורפאתיו". כל הרשעים והמומרים וכיוצא
בהן שחזרו בתשובה בין בגלוי בין במטמוניות מקבלין אותן, שנאמר
"שובו בנים שובבים", אף על פי שעדיין שובב הוא שהרי שב בסתר
ולא בגלוי מקבלין אותו בתשובה.

Nothing can stand in the way of teshuvah. *Even if he denies G-d's existence throughout his life and repents in his final moments, he merits a portion in the World to Come, as implied by the verse, "'Peace, peace, to the distant and the near,' declares G-d. 'I will heal him.'" Any wicked person, apostate, or the like, who repents, whether in an open, revealed manner or in private, will be accepted as implied by the verse, "Return, faithless children." [We may infer] that even if one is still faithless, as obvious from the fact that he repents in private and not in public, his* teshuvah *will be accepted.*

On the Essence of a Jew

TEXT 11

Babylonian Talmud, Ibid.

שובו בנים שובבים - חוץ מאחר.

"Return O lost children—except for Acher."

Jerusalem Talmud, Ibid.

שובו בנים שובבים - מאלישע בן אבויה.

"Return O lost children—except for Elisha ben Abuya."

TEXT 12

Rabbi Chaim Chizkiyah Medini, Sdei Chemed, vol. 2 p. 127

תלמוד בבלי כי פליג עם הירישלמי נקיטינן כבבלי כנודע היינו
אפילו היכא למיקל.

When the Babylonian Talmud disagrees with the Jerusalem Talmud, the accepted tradition is that the halachah sides with the Babylonian tradition—even when the latter is more lenient.

Recognizing Your Goodness

TEXT 13

Rabbi Yosef Yitzchak Schneersohn
(Rayatz, Frierdiker Rebbe, Previous Rebbe)
1880–1950

Chasidic rebbe, prolific writer, and Jewish activist. Rabbi Yosef Yitzchak, the 6th leader of the Chabad movement, actively promoted Jewish religious practice in Soviet Russia and was arrested for these activities. After his release from prison and exile, he settled in Warsaw, Poland, from where he fled Nazi occupation, and arrived in New York in 1940. Settling in Brooklyn, Rabbi Schneersohn worked to revitalize American Jewish life. His son-in law, Rabbi Menachem Mendel Schneerson, succeeded him as the leader of the Chabad movement.

Rabbi Yosef Yitzchak Schneersohn of Lubavitch, Sefer Hasichot 5710 p. 386

אזוי ווי מען דארף וויסן די חסרונות, אזוי דארף מען וויסן די
אייגינע מעלות.

Just as one must recognize shortcomings, so, too, one must recognize his own good qualities.

TEXT 14

The Lubavitcher Rebbe, Torat Menachem 5742 vol. 1 p. 53-54

לפעמים מנסה היצר הרע לבלבל יהודי מעשיית התשובה – על ידי זה שמסביר לו את גודל חסרונותיו, ומסביר לו שבהיותו במעמד ומצב גרוע כזה הרי זה כבר מקרה אבוד, ולא יוכל להיטיב את דרכו כו', ולכן—מציע היצר הרע—כדאי לו לכל הפחות להנות מעניני עולם הזה.

ולכן, צריך להזהר מעצת היצר—שלא ליפול ברוחו ח"ו, בידעו שזוהי תחבולת היצר לבלבלו מעבודת התשובה.

וכידוע פתגם רבותינו נשיאינו "כשם שצריכים לידע את החסרונות, כמו כן צריכים לידע מעלות עצמו". ובזה ישנו דיוק נפלא: כאשר מדובר אודות המעלות—הלשון הוא "מעלות עצמו", ואילו כאשר מדובר אודות החסרונות—הלשון הוא "חסרונות" סתם, ולא חסרונות עצמו!

והביאור בזה...

יהודי מצד עצמו אינו שייך לענין של חטא כלל, וגם כאשר נכשל בענין של חטא ח"ו—אין זה חסרון עצמו, אלא זהו דבר שמחוץ הימנו שנדבק אליו, זאת אומרת: היות שהוא נמצא בעולם הזה הגשמי והחומרי... שצריך לעסוק ולפעול בעולם... יתכן שנדבק אצלו משהו מגשמיות וחומריות העולם. ולכן, אף על פי שזהו "חסרון", אין זה חסרון עצמו, כי חסרון זה אינו מצד עצמו, אלא מצד מציאות העולם שמסביבו.

ולכן, אינו נופל ברוחו ח"ו, בידעו שהחסרון הוא דבר שמחוץ הימנו שנדבק בו. אבל לאידך—יודע הוא שתפקידו לתקן חסרון זה על ידי עבודת התשובה.

Rabbi Menachem Mendel Schneerson
1902–1994

The towering Jewish leader of the 20th century, known as "the Lubavitcher Rebbe," or simply as "the Rebbe." Born in southern Ukraine, the Rebbe escaped Nazi-occupied Europe, arriving in the U.S. in June 1941. The Rebbe inspired and guided the revival of traditional Judaism after the European devastation, impacting virtually every Jewish community the world over. The Rebbe often emphasized that the performance of just one additional good deed could usher in the era of Mashiach. The Rebbe's scholarly talks and writings have been printed in more than 200 volumes.

The yetzer hara *sometimes tries to obstruct a Jew from doing* teshuvah. *A classic tactic is to demonstrate to the person the extent of his deficiency; now, if he's such a delinquent anyway, with no hope of improvement, he may as well enjoy himself and partake of some worldly pleasures.*

Accordingly, one must be vigilant against such plots and avoid all sense of despair. One ought to know that these are merely the wily schemes of the yetzer hara *to obstruct the path to* teshuvah.

Our Rebbe's statement is well known, "Just as one must recognize shortcomings, so, too, one must recognize his own good qualities." There is a wonderful insight one can glean from the nuanced language: When speaking of the qualities, the language is "his own good qualities," whereas when discussing the shortcomings, the language is simply "shortcomings," not referring to them as "his" shortcomings.

The explanation is as follows…

A Jew is inherently distant from sin. Even in those instances where he or she does sin, it does not become "his" or "her" shortcoming, rather it is as an external matter that has become attached to him or her.

In other words: Inasmuch as a Jew lives in a material world… and is tasked with the mission to engage with it… it is possible for some of the materialism and negativity of the world to become attached to him. Thus, though it may indeed be a shortcoming, it is not "his" shortcoming, for it really stems from the material world around him.

In light of the above, a Jew should not let his spirit down, armed with the knowledge that all shortcomings are in reality independent agents that have attached to him. Conversely, he ought to be motivated to teshuvah *to repair these shortcomings.*

What Moses Didn't Know

Capturing the Core of the Jew

*Dedicated in honor of the birthday of our friend **Rabbi Nochum Schapiro**, 18 Tishrei.*
May he and his family merit to witness the fulfillment of continuous blessings
for health, happiness, nachas and success in all their endeavors.

OVERVIEW
Simchat Torah

The holiday of Sukkot is followed by an independent holiday called Shemini Atzeret. In Israel, this is a one-day holiday; in the Diaspora it is a two-day holiday, and the second day is known as Simchat Torah. This holiday is characterized by utterly unbridled joy, which surpasses even the joy of Sukkot. The joy reaches its climax on Simchat Torah, when we celebrate the conclusion—and restart—of the annual Torah-reading cycle.

These two days constitute a major holiday, when most forms of work are prohibited. The special joy of this holiday celebrates the conclusion—and restart—of the annual Torah-reading cycle On the preceding nights, women and girls light candles, reciting the appropriate blessings, and we enjoy nightly and daily festive meals, accompanied by kiddush. We don't go to work, drive, write, or switch on or off electric devices. We are permitted to cook and to carry outdoors (unless it is also Shabbat).

The first day, Shemini Atzeret, features the prayer for rain, officially commemorating the start of the Mediterranean (i.e., Israeli) rainy season, and the Yizkor prayer (supplicating G-d to remember the souls of the departed).

We no longer take the Four Kinds, and we no longer mention Sukkot in the day's prayers; in the Diaspora, however, we do still eat in the sukkah (but without reciting the blessing on it).

The highlight of the second day, Simchat Torah ("The Joy of the Torah"), is the hakafot, held on both the eve and the morning of Simchat Torah, in which we march and dance with the Torah scrolls around the reading table in the synagogue. (In many synagogues, hakafot are conducted also on the eve of Shemini Atzeret.)

On this joyous day when we conclude the Torah, it is customary for every man to take part in the celebration by receiving an aliyah. The children, too, receive an aliyah!

After the final aliyah of the Torah, we immediately begin a new cycle from the beginning of Genesis (from a second Torah scroll); this is because as soon as we conclude studying the Torah, G-d's infinite wisdom, on one level, we immediately start again, this time to discover new and loftier interpretations.

(In the Land of Israel, the celebration and customs of these two days are compressed into one day.)

A Mysterious Festival

TEXT 1

Glosses of Rema to Shulchan Aruch Orach Chaim, 669

וקורין יום טוב האחרון שמחת תורה, לפי ששמחין ועושין בו סעודת משתה לגמרה של תורה. ונוהגין שהמסיים התורה והמתחיל בראשית נודרים נדבות וקוראים לאחרים לעשות משתה.

ועוד נהגו במדינות אלו להוציא בשמחת תורה ערבית ושחרית כל ספרי תורה שבהיכל ואומרים זמירות ותשבחות, וכל מקום לפי מנהגו.

ועוד נהגו להקיף עם ספרי התורה הבימה שבבית הכנסת, כמו שמקיפים עם הלולב, והכל משום שמחה.

The final day of the festival is called "Simchat Torah," inasmuch as we celebrate and make a festive meal to mark the completion of the Torah. It is customary that the person who merits to conclude the Torah as well as the person who merits to read the first portion of Genesis (Bereishit) donate and call upon others to make a festive meal.

It is also customary in these parts to take all the Torahs out in the evening and the morning and to sings songs—each place according to its custom.

Another custom is to surround the bimah *with the Torah scrolls from the synagogue, as we do with the lulav [on Sukkot]. All of this is done to increase joy.*

TEXT 2

Rabbi Yisrael Meir Kagan of Radin, *Mishnah Berurah* ad loc.

כתב מהרי"ק בשם רב האי גאון בשורש ט' "יום זה רגילים אצלנו
לרקד בו אפילו כמה זקנים בשעה שאומרים קילוסים לתורה וכו'".
ולכן יש להתאמץ בזה לרקד ולזמר לכבוד התורה כמו שכתוב גבי
דוד המלך ע"ה "מפזז ומכרכר בכל עוז לפני ה'", וכן כתבו משם
האר"י ז"ל.

והעידו על האר"י ז"ל שאמר שהמעלה העליונה שהשיג באה לו
על די שהיה משמח בכל עוז בשמחה של מצוה וגם על הגר"א ז"ל
כתבו שהיה מרקד לפני הספר תורה בכל כחו.

Rabbi Yisrael Meir Hakohen Kagan (*Chafets Chayim*) 1839–1933
Pre-WWII Polish Halachist and ethicist. Rabbi Kagan was the dean of the illustrious yeshivah in Radin, Poland. A prolific author on topics of Halachah and ethical behavior, he is often called *Chafets Chayim* after his first work, a comprehensive digest of laws pertaining to ethical speech. His magnum opus, on which he worked for 28 years, is *Mishnah Berurah*, a concise commentary on the first section of the Shulchan Aruch. He also authored *Bi'ur Halachah* on the Shulchan Aruch and numerous other works.

It is cited in the name of Rabbi Hai Gaon, "We are accustomed to dancing on this day. Even the elderly participate in the festivities, praising the Torah."

Thus, one ought to invest energy and dance and sing to the honor of the Torah, as it is stated regarding King David, "…hopping and dancing before G-d." The Arizal is cited similarly.

The Arizal said that the gates of wisdom and Divine inspiration were opened for him only as a reward for doing mitzvot with boundless joy. It is said about the great Gaon of Vilna that he, too, would dance with all his might in front of the Torah.

Different Ancient Practices

Babylonian Talmud
A literary work of monumental proportions that draws upon the legal, spiritual, intellectual, ethical, and historical traditions of Judaism. The 37 tractates of the Babylonian Talmud contain the teachings of the Jewish sages from the period after the destruction of the 2nd Temple through the 5th century CE. It has served as the primary vehicle for the transmission of the Oral Law and the education of Jews over the centuries; it is the entry point for all subsequent legal, ethical, and theological Jewish scholarship.

TEXT 3

Talmud Tractate Megillah, 29b

בני מערבא דמסקי לדאורייתא בתלת שנין (מסיימין חמשה חומשין פעם אחת לשלש שנים, ולא בכל שנה כמו שאנו עושין. –רש"י).

The people of the West conclude the Torah every three years (they conclude the Five Books one time over the course of three years, not every year as we do. – Rashi)

Torah Studies Season Four 5777

TEXT 4

Maimonides, Laws of Prayer and the Priestly Blessing, 13:1

המנהג הפשוט בכל ישראל שמשלימין את התורה בשנה אחת,
מתחילין בשבת שאחר חג הסוכות וקורין בסדר בראשית... וקוראין
והולכין על הסדר הזה עד שגומרין את התורה בחג הסוכות, ויש מי
שמשלימים את התורה בשלש שנים ואינו מנהג פשוט.

The common custom throughout all Israel is to complete the [reading of] the Torah in one year. [The cycle] begins on the Shabbat after the Sukkot festival, reading the sidrah Bereishit... We continue reading according to this order until the Torah is completed, during the Sukkot festival. There are those who finish the Torah reading in a three-year cycle. However, this is not a widely accepted custom.

Rabbi Moshe ben Maimon
(Maimonides, Rambam)
1135–1204
Halachist, philosopher, author, and physician. Maimonides was born in Cordoba, Spain. After the conquest of Cordoba by the Almohads, he fled Spain and eventually settled in Cairo, Egypt. There, he became the leader of the Jewish community and served as court physician to the vizier of Egypt. He is most noted for authoring the *Mishneh Torah*, an encyclopedic arrangement of Jewish law, and for his philosophical work, *Guide for the Perplexed*. His rulings on Jewish law are integral to the formation of halachic consensus.

TEXT 5

Otzar HaGe'onim, Tractate Megillah p. 62

יש מנהג כי ביום הכפורים בעת מנחה אומר מן בראשית עד יום
אחד על פה. ומביאים ראיה כי כל עשרת ימי תשובה השטן עומד
להשטין את ישראל ואומר הרי התורה שנתת לישראל כבר גמרו
אותה, וכאשר הקדוש ברוך הוא שומע שהתחילו מבראשית מיד
גוער בשטן ואומר לו הלא ראית כי מיד שגמרו התחילו מרוב
אהבתם את תורתי. מיד ידום השטן בעל כרחו וכו'.

There is a custom to recite the verses from "Bereishit..." until "...one day." They cite support for this custom from the fact that the entire Ten Days of Penitence the Satan seeks to prosecute the Jews, arguing, "Look! —The Jews are finished with the Torah that you gave them!" When G-d hears the Jews starting anew from Bereishit, He immediately chastises the Satan and exclaims, "Don't you see—the Jews have immediately restarted the Torah for they love it so much!" Immediately, the Satan is forcibly silenced.

Beginnings of a Festival

TEXT 6

Rabbi Aharon Hakohen of Narbonne, Sefer Kolbo ch. 20

יום תשיעי הוא יום שמחת תורה והמנהג שקורין בו וזאת הברכה
שהוא סיום התורה ושמחין בו שמחה גדולה ולהרבות השמחה נהגו
לקרות יותר ממנין הקורין ולהוסיף עליהן... ושמנה פסוקים שבסוף
הסדר שהם מויעל משה עד ויהושע יחיד קורא אותן כמו שכתבנו
למעלה. ובשניה קורא המפטיר כאתמול... ואחר ההפטרה אומרים
אשרי ואחר כך עומדים על המגדל עם ספר התורה, גם נהגו להוסיף
להוציא כל ספרי התורה אשר בתיבה ולעמד על המגדל כל הזקנים
וספר תורה בזרועם ומקוננים כל אחד על פטירת משה רבן של
נביאים ומזכירין לטובה כל מי שנדבו לבו להקדיש ולעשות צדקה

The ninth day is the festival of Simchat Torah. The custom is to read the parashah *of Vezot Habrachah, which is the final passage of the Torah. We are exceedingly joyous on this day, and the custom is to call up more people than usual to the Torah… The last eight verses are read by a distinguished person, and the* maftir *is read from the second scroll… After the* haftorah, *Ashrei is recited, and then the congregation stands on the podium with the scrolls. There is also a custom to take out all of the scrolls from the Ark and for the elderly to stand with them on the podium. The assembled mourn the death of Moses, the master of all prophets, and anyone who has donated to the honor of G-d as well as the deceased is given an honorary mention. Prayers are recited for the entire Jewish nation. Thereafter, the scrolls are returned to the Ark and the Musaf prayer is recited.*

Hakafot

TEXT 7

Talmud Tractate Sukkah, 45a

מצות ערבה כיצד? מקום היה למטה מירושלים ונקרא מוצא. יורדין לשם ומלקטין משם מורביות של ערבה, ובאין וזוקפין אותן בצדי המזבח, וראשיהן כפופין על גבי המזבח. תקעו והריעו ותקעו. בכל יום מקיפין את המזבח פעם אחת, ואומרים אנא ה' הושיעה נא, אנא ה' הצליחה נא. רבי יהודה אומר: אני והו הושיעה נא. ואותו היום מקיפין את המזבח שבע פעמים.

How was the precept of the willow-branch [carried out]? There was a place below Jerusalem called Moza. They went down there and gathered thence young willow-branches and then came and fixed them at the sides of the altar so that their tops bent over the altar. They then sounded a teki'ah [long blast], a teru'ah [tremulous blast], and again a teki'ah. Every day they went round the altar once, saying, "We beseech Thee, O G-d, save now, we beseech thee, O G-d, make us now to prosper." Rabbi Yehudah said, [they were saying], "ani ve-hu, save now." But on that day [hosha'anah rabah] they went round the altar seven times.

TEXT 8

Midrash Yalkut Shimoni, Tehillim ch. 703

ואותו היום היו מקיפין שבע פעמים. אמר ר' חייא זכר ליריחו, הא
תינח בזמן שיש מזבח, בזמן הזה חזן הכנסת עומד כמלאך האלהים
וספר תורה בזרועו, והעם מקיפין אותו דוגמת מזבח.

*They would make seven circuits on that day. Rabbi
Chiya said it commemorates Jericho during the times
when there is an altar. In the current era, the leader
of the congregation stands like an angel with a Torah
scroll in his arm, and the congregation makes circuits
similar to the altar.*

Yalkut Shimoni

A Midrash that covers the
entire Biblical text. Its
material is collected from
all over rabbinic literature,
including the Babylonian
and Jerusalem Talmuds and
various ancient Midrashic
texts. It contains several
passages from Midrashim
that have been lost, as well
as different versions of
existing Midrashim. It is
unclear when and by whom
this Midrash was redacted.

Between Moses and Rabbi Akiva

The Crowns

TEXT 9

Talmud Tractate Menachot, 29b

אמר רב יהודה אמר רב, בשעה שעלה משה למרום מצאו להקדוש
ברוך הוא שיושב וקושר כתרים לאותיות. אמר לפניו "רבונו של
עולם מי מעכב על ידך?"
אמר לו "אדם אחד יש שעתיד להיות בסוף כמה דורות ועקיבא בן
יוסף שמו שעתיד לדרוש על כל קוץ וקוץ תילין תילין של הלכות".
אמר לפניו " רבונו של עולם הראהו לי".
אמר לו "חזור לאחורך".
הלך וישב בסוף שמונה שורות ולא היה יודע מה הן אומרים. תשש
כחו. כיון שהגיע לדבר אחד, אמרו לו תלמידיו "רבי מנין לך?" אמר
להן "הלכה למשה מסיני". נתיישבה דעתו.

*Rabbi Yehuda said in the name of Rav: When Moses
ascended to heaven during his stay on Mount Sinai,
he found the Holy One, blessed be He, affixing crowns,
thin lines, to the letters [of the Torah].*

*Moses asked G-d, "Master of the Universe, what is
lacking in the words themselves that You must add
crowns as well?"*

G-d answered, "There will arise a man, after many generations, Akiva son of Joseph is his name, who will expound upon each of these lines—upon each of these crowns—heaps upon heaps of laws."

Moses asked G-d, "Master of the Universe, show him to me."

G-d responded, "Retreat backwards."

Moses went and sat at the edge of the eighth row [of Rabbi Akiva's lecture hall]. And could not understand what they were saying. They arrived at a certain matter, and Moses heard the students asking Rabbi Akiva, "How do you know that?" When Rabbi Akiva replied, "It is a tradition from Moses at Sinai," Moses was relieved.

Between Moses and Rabbi Akiva

TEXT 10

Talmud Tractate Sotah, 12a

אחרים אומרים: נולד כשהוא מהול; וחכמים אומרים: בשעה שנולד משה נתמלא הבית כולו אור.

Others say: He was born circumcised; and the Sages declare: At the time when Moses was born, the whole house was filled with light.

TEXT 11

Talmud Tractate Pesachim, 49b

אמר רבי עקיבא: כשהייתי עם הארץ אמרתי: מי יתן לי תלמיד חכם
ואנשכנו כחמור.

Rabbi Akiva said: When I was an ignoramus, I would say, "Give me a Torah scholar and I will bite him as a donkey bites."

Two Holidays

TEXT 12

Talmud Tractate Yoma, 85b

אמר רבי עקיבא: אשריכם ישראל, לפני מי אתם מטהרין, מי מטהר
אתכם - אביכם שבשמים, שנאמר "וזרקתי עליכם מים טהורים
וטהרתם" ואומר "מקוה ישראל (ה')" מה מקוה מטהר את הטמאים
- אף הקדוש ברוך הוא מטהר את ישראל.

Rabbi Akiva said, Happy are you, Israel! Before whom is it that you are purified and who purifies you? Your Father in Heaven … Just as a fountain purifies the impure, so does the Holy One, blessed be He, purify Israel.

The Simchat Torah Jew

Ink in the Quill

TEXT 13

Midrash Shemot Rabah, 47:11

מנין זכה משה לקרני ההוד?...

רב שמואל אמר עד שמשה כותב את התורה נשתייר בקולמוס
קמעא והעבירו על ראשו וממנו נעשו לו קרני ההוד.

On what basis did Moshe merit the unique beams
of glory?...

Rabbi Shmuel said: When he was writing the original
Torah scroll [which G-d dictated], there was a little
drop of ink left over. G-d took that ink and rubbed it
on Moshe's head. The beams of glory were the result
of that drop of ink.

Shemot Rabah
An early rabbinic commentary
on the Book of Exodus.
Midrash is the designation of
a particular genre of rabbinic
literature usually forming
a running commentary on
specific books of the Bible.
Shemot Rabah, written
mostly in Hebrew, provides
textual exegeses, expounds
upon the biblical narrative,
and develops and illustrates
moral principles. It was first
printed in Constantinople in
1512 together with four other
midrashic works on the other
four books of the Pentateuch.

The Source of Hakafot

Rabbi Menachem Mendel Schneerson
1902–1994

The towering Jewish leader of the 20th century, known as "the Lubavitcher Rebbe," or simply as "the Rebbe." Born in southern Ukraine, the Rebbe escaped Nazi-occupied Europe, arriving in the U.S. in June 1941. The Rebbe inspired and guided the revival of traditional Judaism after the European devastation, impacting virtually every Jewish community the world over. The Rebbe often emphasized that the performance of just one additional good deed could usher in the era of Mashiach. The Rebbe's scholarly talks and writings have been printed in more than 200 volumes.

TEXT 14

The Lubavitcher Rebbe, Likutei Sichot, vol. 34 p. 223

בשמחת תורה מודגשת ומתגלה מעלתן של ישראל... היינו, שהענין דשמחת תורה הוא—"יהיו לך לבדך ואין לזרים אתך", ובלשון הזהר—"לא אשתכח במלכא אלא ישראל בלחודוהי".

The supreme quality of a Jew is expressed on Simchat Torah... In other words, the joy of Simchat Torah is this that "We are Yours alone, and there is no place for foreigners with You," or in the words of the Zohar, "Only the Jews are found together with the King."